... in the case where the self is merely represented and ideally presented (*vorgestellt*), there it is not actual: where it is by proxy, it *is* not.

—Hegel, *Phenomenology of Mind*

Guy Debord

SOCIETY
OF THE SPECTACLE

Black & Red
Detroit
1983

La societé du spectacle was first published in 1967 by Editions Buchet-Chastel (Paris); it was reprinted in 1971 by Champ Libre (Paris).

The first English translation was pubished by Black & Red in 1970. It was revised in 1977, incorporating numerous improvements suggested by friends and critics of the first translation.

Guy Debord was editor of the journal *Internationale Situationniste* from 1958 to 1969. He died in 1994.

No copyright
No rights reserved

Reprinted in 2018

ISBN 0-934868-07-7
ISBN-13 978-0-934868-07-5

Available from:

Black & Red
PO Box 02374
Detroit, Michigan 48202

and

AK Press
370 Ryan Ave #100
Chico, California 95973
www.akpress.org

Contents

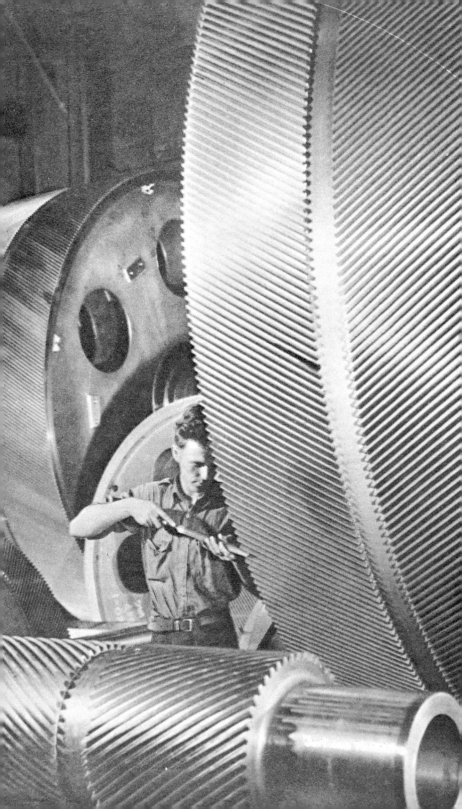

I

Separation Perfected

But certainly for the present age, which prefers
the sign to the thing signified, the copy to the
original, fancy to reality, the appearance to the
essence, . . . *illusion* only is *sacred, truth pro-*
fane. Nay, sacredness is held to be enhanced in
proportion as truth decreases and illusion increases, so that the highest degree of illusion
comes to be the highest degree of sacredness.

—Feuerbach, Preface to the Second Edition
of *The Essence of Christianity*

1

In societies where modern conditions of production prevail, all of life presents itself as an immense accumulation of *spectacles*. Everything that was directly lived has moved away into a representation.

2

The images detached from every aspect of life fuse in a common stream in which the unity of this life can no longer be reestablished. Reality considered *partially* unfolds, in its own general unity, as a pseudo-world *apart*, an object of mere contemplation. The specialization of images of the world is completed in the world of the autonomous image, where the liar has lied to himself. The spectacle in general, as the concrete inversion of life, is the autonomous movement of the non-living.

3

The spectacle presents itself simultaneously as all of society, as part of society, and as *instrument of unification*. As a part of society it is specifically the sector which concentrates all gazing and all consciousness. Due to the very fact that this sector is *separate*, it is the common ground of the deceived gaze and of false consciousness, and the unification it achieves is nothing but an official language of generalized separation.

4

The spectacle is not a collection of images, but a social relation among people, mediated by images.

5

The spectacle cannot be understood as an abuse of the world of vision, as a product of the techniques of mass dissemination of images. It is, rather, a *Weltanschauung* which has become actual, materially translated. It is a world vision which has become objectified.

The spectacle, grasped in its totality, is both the result and the project of the existing mode of production. It is not a supplement to the real world, an additional decoration. It is the heart of the unrealism of the real society. In all its specific forms, as information or propaganda, as advertisement or direct entertainment consumption, the spectacle is the present *model* of socially dominant life. It is the omnipresent affirmation of the choice *already made* in production and its corollary consumption. The spectacle's form and content are identically the total justification of the existing system's conditions and goals. The spectacle is also the *permanent presence* of this justification, since it occupies the main part of the time lived outside of modern production.

7

Separation is itself part of the unity of the world, of the global social praxis split up into reality and image. The social practice which the autonomous spectacle confronts is also the real totality which contains the spectacle. But the split within this totality mutilates it to the point of making the spectacle appear as its goal. The language of the spectacle consists of *signs* of the ruling production, which at the same time are the ultimate goal of this production.

8

One cannot abstractly contrast the spectacle to actual social activity: such a division is itself divided. The spectacle which inverts the real is in fact produced. Lived reality is materially invaded by the contemplation of the spectacle while simultaneously absorbing the spectacular order, giving it positive cohesiveness. Objective reality is present on both sides. Every notion fixed this way has no other basis than its passage into the opposite: reality rises up within the spectacle, and the spectacle is real. This reciprocal alienation is the essence and the support of the existing society.

In a world which *really is topsy-turvy*, the true is a moment of the false.

The concept of "spectacle" unifies and explains a great diversity of apparent phenomena. The diversity and the contrasts are appearances of a socially organized appearance, the general truth of which must itself be recognized. Considered in its own terms, the spectacle is *affirmation* of appearance and affirmation of all human life, namely social life, as mere appearance. But the critique which reaches the truth of the spectacle exposes it as the visible *negation* of life, as a negation of life which *has become visible*.

To describe the spectacle, its formation, its functions and the forces which tend to dissolve it, one must artificially distinguish certain inseparable elements. When *analyzing* the spectacle one speaks, to some extent, the language of the spectacular itself in the sense that one moves through the methodological terrain of the very society which expresses itself in the spectacle. But the spectacle is nothing other than the *sense* of the total practice of a social-economic formation, its *use of time*. It is the historical movement in which we are caught.

The spectacle presents itself as something enormously positive, indisputable and inaccessible. It says nothing more than "that which appears is good, that which is good appears." The attitude which it demands in principle is passive acceptance which in fact it already obtained by its manner of appearing without reply, by its monopoly of appearance.

The basically tautological character of the spectacle flows from the simple fact that its means are simultaneously its ends.

It is the sun which never sets over the empire of modern passivity. It covers the entire surface of the world and bathes endlessly in its own glory.

14

The society which rests on modern industry is not accidentally or superficially spectacular, it is fundamentally *spectaclist*. In the spectacle, which is the image of the ruling economy, the goal is nothing, development everything. The spectacle aims at nothing other than itself.

15

As the indispensable decoration of the objects produced today, as the general exposé of the rationality of the system, as the advanced economic sector which directly shapes a growing multitude of image-objects, the spectacle is the *main production* of present-day society.

16

The spectacle subjugates living men to itself to the extent that the economy has totally subjugated them. It is no more than the economy developing for itself. It is the true reflection of the production of things, and the false objectification of the producers.

17

The first phase of the domination of the economy over social life brought into the definition of all human realization the obvious degradation of *being* into *having*. The present phase of total occupation of social life by the accumulated results of the economy leads to a generalized sliding of *having* into *appearing*, from which all actual "having" must draw its immediate prestige and its ultimate function. At the same time all individual reality has become social reality directly dependent on social power and shaped by it. It is allowed to appear only to the extent that it *is not*.

Where the real world changes into simple images, the simple images become real beings and effective motivations of hypnotic behavior. The spectacle, as a tendency *to make one see* the world by means of various specialized mediations (it can no longer be grasped directly), naturally finds vision to be the privileged human sense which the sense of touch was for other epochs; the most abstract, the most mystifiable sense corresponds to the generalized abstraction of present-day society. But the spectacle is not identifiable with mere gazing, even combined with hearing. It is that which escapes the activity of men, that which escapes reconsideration and correction by their work. It is the opposite of dialogue. Wherever there is independent *representation*, the spectacle reconstitutes itself.

The spectacle inherits all the *weaknesses* of the Western philosophical project which undertook to comprehend activity in terms of the categories of *seeing*; furthermore, it is based on the incessant spread of the precise technical rationality which grew out of this thought. The spectacle does not realize philosophy, it philosophizes reality. The concrete life of everyone has been degraded into a *speculative* universe.

Philosophy, the power of separate thought and the thought of separate power, could never by itself supersede theology. The spectacle is the material reconstruction of the religious illusion. Spectacular technology has not dispelled the religious clouds where men had placed their own powers detached from themselves; it has only tied them to an earthly base. The most earthly life thus becomes opaque and unbreathable. It no longer projects into the sky but shelters within itself its absolute denial, its fallacious paradise. The spectacle is the technical realization of the exile of human powers into a beyond; it is separation perfected within the interior of man.

21

To the extent that necessity is socially dreamed, the dream becomes necessary. The spectacle is the nightmare of imprisoned modern society which ultimately expresses nothing more than its desire to sleep. The spectacle is the guardian of sleep.

22

The fact that the practical power of modern society detached itself and built an independent empire in the spectacle

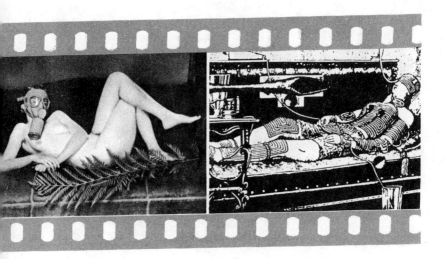

can be explained only by the fact that this practical power continued to lack cohesion and remained in contradiction with itself.

23

The oldest social specialization, the specialization of power, is at the root of the spectacle. The spectacle is thus a specialized activity which speaks for all the others. It is the diplomatic representation of hierarchic society to itself, where all other expression is banned. Here the most modern is also the most archaic.

24

The spectacle is the existing order's uninterrupted discourse about itself, its laudatory monologue. It is the self-portrait of power in the epoch of its totalitarian management of the conditions of existence. The fetishistic, purely objective appearance of spectacular relations conceals the fact that they are relations among men and classes: a second nature with its fatal laws seems to dominate our environment. But the spectacle is not the necessary product of technical development seen as a *natural* development. The society of the spectacle is on the contrary the form which chooses its own technical content. If the spectacle, taken in the limited sense of "mass media" which are its most glaring superficial manifestation, seems to invade society as mere equipment, this equipment is in no way neutral but is the very means suited to its total self-movement. If the social needs of the epoch in which such techniques are developed can only be satisfied through their mediation, if the administration of this society and all contact among men can no longer take place except through the intermediary of this power of instantaneous communication, it is because this "communication" is essentially *unilateral*. The concentration of "communication" is thus an accumulation, in the hands of the existing system's administration, of the means which allow it to carry on this particular administration. The generalized cleavage of the spectacle is inseparable from the modern *State*, namely from the general form of cleavage within society, the product of the division of social labor and the organ of class domination.

Separation is the alpha and omega of the spectacle. The institutionalization of the social division of labor, the formation of classes, had given rise to a first sacred contemplation, the mythical order with which every power shrouds itself from the beginning. The sacred has justified the cosmic and ontological order which corresponded to the interests of the masters; it has explained and embellished that which society *could not do*. Thus all separate power has been spectacular, but the adherence of all to an immobile image only signified the common acceptance of an imaginary prolongation of the poverty of real social activity, still largely felt as a unitary condition. The modern spectacle, on the contrary, expresses what society *can do*, but in this expression the *permitted* is absolutely opposed to the *possible*. The spectacle is the preservation of unconsciousness within the practical change of the conditions of existence. It is its own product, and it has made its own rules: it is a pseudo-sacred entity. It shows what it *is*: separate power developing in itself, in the growth of productivity by means of the incessant refinement of the division of labor into a parcellization of gestures which are then dominated by the independent movement of machines; and working for an ever-expanding market. All community and all critical sense are dissolved during this movement in which the forces that could grow by separating are not yet *reunited*.

26

With the generalized separation of the worker and his products, every unitary view of accomplished activity and all direct personal communication among producers are lost. Accompanying the progress of accumulation of separate products and the concentration of the productive process, unity and communication become the exclusive attribute of the system's management. The success of the economic system of separation is the *proletarianization* of the world.

27

Due to the success of separate production as production of the separate, the fundamental experience which in primitive societies is attached to a central task is in the process of being displaced, at the crest of the system's development, by non-work, by inactivity. But this inactivity is in no way liberated from productive activity: it depends on productive activity and is an uneasy and admiring submission to the necessities and results of production; it is itself a product of its rationality. There can be no freedom outside of activity, and in the context of the spectacle all activity is negated, just as real activity has been captured in its entirety for the global construction of this result. Thus the present "liberation from labor," the increase of leisure, is in no way a liberation within labor, nor a liberation from the world shaped by this labor. None of the activity lost in labor can be regained in the submission to its result.

28

The economic system founded on isolation is a *circular production of isolation*. The technology is based on isolation, and the technical process isolates in turn. From the automobile to television, all the *goods selected* by the spectacular system are also its weapons for a constant reinforcement of the conditions of isolation of "lonely crowds." The spectacle constantly rediscovers its own assumptions more concretely.

29

The spectacle originates in the loss of the unity of the world, and the gigantic expansion of the modern spectacle expresses the totality of this loss: the abstraction of all specific labor and the general abstraction of the entirety of production are perfectly rendered in the spectacle, whose *mode of being concrete* is precisely abstraction. In the spectacle, one part of the world *represents itself* to the world and is superior to it. The spectacle is nothing more than the common language of this separation. What binds the spectators together is no more than an irreversible relation at the very center which maintains their isolation. The spectacle reunites the separate, but reunites it *as separate*.

30

The alienation of the spectator to the profit of the contemplated object (which is the result of his own unconscious ac-

tivity) is expressed in the following way: the more he contemplates the less he lives; the more he accepts recognizing
himself in the dominant images of need, the less he under-
stands his own existence and his own desires. The externality
of the spectacle in relation to the active man appears in the fact
that his own gestures are no longer his but those of another
who represents them to him. This is why the spectator feels at
home nowhere, because the spectacle is everywhere.

31

The worker does not produce himself; he produces an independent power. The *success* of this production, its abundance, returns to the producer as an *abundance of dispossession*. All the time and space of his world become
foreign to him with the accumulation of his alienated products.
The spectacle is the map of this new world, a map which exactly covers its territory. The very powers which escaped us
show themselves to us in all their force.

32

The spectacle within society corresponds to a concrete
manufacture of alienation. Economic expansion is mainly the
expansion of this specific industrial production. What grows
with the economy in motion for itself can only be the very alienation which was at its origin.

33

Separated from his product, man himself produces all the
details of his world with ever increasing power, and thus finds
himself ever more separated from his world. The more his life
is now his product, the more he is separated from his life.

34

The spectacle is *capital* to such a degree of accumulation
that it becomes an image.

II

The Commodity as Spectacle

The commodity can only be understood in its undistorted essence when it becomes the universal category of society as a whole. Only in this context does the reification produced by commodity relations assume decisive importance both for the objective evolution of society and for the stance adopted by men towards it. Only then does the commodity become crucial for the subjugation of men's consciousness to the forms in which this reification finds expression. . . As labor is progressively rationalized and mechanized, his (the worker's) lack of will is reinforced by the way in which his activity becomes less and less active and more and more *contemplative.*

—Lukacs, *History and Class Consciousness*

In the essential movement of the spectacle, which consists of taking up all that existed in human activity *in a fluid state* so as to possess it in a congealed state as things which have become the exclusive value by their *formulation in negative* of lived value, we recognize our old enemy, *the commodity*, who knows so well how to seem at first glance something trivial and obvious, while on the contrary it is so complex and so full of metaphysical subtleties.

36

This is the principle of commodity fetishism, the domination of society by "intangible as well as tangible things," which reaches its absolute fulfillment in the spectacle, where the tangible world is replaced by a selection of images which exist above it, and which simultaneously impose themselves as the tangible *par excellence.*

37

The world at once present and absent which the spectacle *makes visible* is the world of the commodity dominating all that is lived. The world of the commodity is thus shown for *what it is,* because its movement is identical to the *estrangement* of men among themselves and in relation to their global product.

38

The loss of quality so evident at all levels of spectacular language, from the objects it praises to the behavior it regulates, merely translates the fundamental traits of the real production which brushes reality aside: the commodity-form is through and through equal to itself, the category of the quantitative. The quantitative is what the commodity-form develops, and it can develop only within the quantitative.

This development which excludes the qualitative is itself, as development, subject to qualitative change: the spectacle indicates that it has crossed the threshold of *its own abundance*; this is as yet true only locally at some points, but is already true on the universal scale which is the original context of the commodity, a context which its practical movement, encompassing the Earth as a world market, has verified.

The development of productive forces has been *the real unconscious history* which built and modified the conditions of existence of human groups as conditions of survival, and extended those conditions: the economic basis of all their undertakings. In a primitive economy, the commodity sector represented a surplus of survival. The production of commodities, which implies the exchange of varied products among independent producers, could for a long time remain craft production, contained within a marginal economic function where its quantitative truth was still masked. However, where commodity production met the social conditions of large scale commerce and of the accumulation of capitals, it seized total domination over the economy. The entire economy then became what the commodity had shown itself to be in the course of this conquest: a process of quantitative development. This incessant expansion of economic power in the form of the commodity, which transformed human labor into commodity-labor, into *wage-labor*, cumulatively led to an abundance in which the primary question of survival is undoubtedly resolved, but in such a way that it is constantly rediscovered; it is continually posed again each time at a higher level. Economic growth frees societies from the natural pressure which required their direct struggle for survival, but at that point it is from their liberator that they are not liberated. The *independence* of the commodity is extended to the entire economy over which it rules. The economy transforms the world, but transforms it only into a world of economy. The pseudo-nature within which human labor is alienated demands that it be *served* ad infinitum, and this service, being judged and absolved only by itself, in fact acquires the totality of socially permissible efforts and projects as its servants. The abundance of commodities, namely, of commodity relations, can be nothing more than *increased survival*.

The commodity's domination was at first exerted over the economy in an occult manner; the economy itself, the material basis of social life, remained unperceived and not understood, like the familiar which is not necessarily known. In a society where the concrete commodity is rare or unusual, money, apparently dominant, presents itself as an emissary armed with full powers who speaks in the name of an unknown force. With the industrial revolution, the division of labor in manufactures, and mass production for the world market, the commodity appears in fact as a power which comes to *occupy* social life. It is then that political economy takes shape, as the dominant science and the science of domination.

The spectacle is the moment when the commodity has attained the *total occupation* of social life. Not only is the relation to the commodity visible but it is all one sees: the world one sees is its world. Modern economic production extends its dictatorship extensively and intensively. In the least industrialized places, its reign is already attested by a few star commodities and by the imperialist domination imposed by regions which are ahead in the development of productivity. In the advanced regions, social space is invaded by a continuous

superimposition of geological layers of commodities. At this point in the "second industrial revolution," alienated consumption becomes for the masses a duty supplementary to alienated production. It is *all the sold labor* of a society which globally becomes the *total commodity* for which the cycle must be continued. For this to be done, the total commodity has to return as a fragment to the fragmented individual, absolutely separated from the productive forces operating as a whole. Thus it is here that the specialized science of domination must in turn specialize: it fragments itself into sociology, psychotechnics, cybernetics, semiology, etc., watching over the self-regulation of every level of the process.

43

Whereas in the primitive phase of capitalist accumulation, "political economy sees in the *proletarian* only the *worker*" who must receive the minimum indispensable for the conservation of his labor power, without ever seeing him "in his leisure and humanity," these ideas of the ruling class are reversed as soon as the production of commodities reaches a level of abundance which requires a surplus of collaboration from the worker. This worker, suddenly redeemed from the total contempt which is clearly shown him by all the varieties of organization and supervision of production, finds himself every day, outside of production and in the guise of a con-

sumer, seemingly treated as an adult, with zealous politeness. At this point the *humanism of the commodity* takes charge of the worker's "leisure and humanity," simply because now political economy can and must dominate these spheres *as political economy*. Thus the "perfected denial of man" has taken charge of the totality of human existence.

44

The spectacle is a permanent opium war which aims to make people identify goods with commodities and satisfaction with survival that increases according to its own laws. But if consumable survival is something which must always increase, this is because it continues *to contain privation*. If there is nothing beyond increasing survival, if there is no point where it might stop growing, this is not because it is beyond privation, but because it is enriched privation.

45

Automation, the most advanced sector of modern industry as well as the model which perfectly sums up its practice, drives the commodity world toward the following contradiction: the technical equipment which objectively eliminates labor must at the same time preserve *labor as a commodity* and as the only source of the commodity. If the social labor (time) engaged by the society is not to diminish because of automation (or any other less extreme form of increasing the productivity of labor), then new jobs have to be created. Services, the tertiary sector, swell the ranks of the army of distribution and are a eulogy to the current commodities; the additional forces which are mobilized just happen to be suitable for the organization of redundant labor required by the artificial needs for such commodities.

46

Exchange value could arise only as an agent of use value, but its victory by means of its own weapons created the conditions for its autonomous domination. Mobilizing all human use and establishing a monopoly over its satisfaction, exchange value has ended up by *directing use.* The process of exchange became identified with all possible use and reduced use to the mercy of exchange. Exchange value is the *condottiere* of use value who ends up waging the war for himself.

47

The tendency of use value to fall, this constant of capitalist economy, develops a new form of privation within increased survival: the new privation is not far removed from the old penury since it requires most men to participate as wage workers in the endless pursuit of its attainment, and since everyone knows he must submit or die. The reality of this blackmail accounts for the general acceptance of the illusion at the heart of the consumption of modern commodities: use in its most impoverished form (food and lodging) today exists only to the extent that it is imprisoned in the illusory wealth of increased survival. The real consumer becomes a consumer of illusions. The commodity is this factually real illusion, and the spectacle is its general manifestation.

48

In the inverted reality of the spectacle, use value (which was implicitly contained in exchange value) must now be explicitly proclaimed precisely because its factual reality is eroded by the overdeveloped commodity economy and because counterfeit life requires a pseudo-justification.

49

The spectacle is the other side of money: it is the general abstract equivalent of all commodities. Money dominated society as the representation of general equivalence, namely, of the exchangeability of different goods whose uses could not be compared. The spectacle is the developed modern complement of money where the totality of the commodity world appears as a whole, as a general equivalence for what the entire society can be and can do. The spectacle is the money which one *only looks at,* because in the spectacle the totality of use is already exchanged for the totality of abstract representation. The spectacle is not only the servant of *pseudo-use,* it is already in itself the pseudo-use of life.

At the moment of *economic* abundance, the concentrated result of social labor becomes visible and subjugates all reality to appearance, which is now its product. Capital is no longer the invisible center which directs the mode of production: its accumulation spreads it all the way to the periphery in the form of tangible objects. The entire expanse of society is its portrait.

51

The victory of the autonomous economy must at the same time be its defeat. The forces which it has unleashed eliminate the *economic necessity* which was the immutable basis of earlier societies. When economic necessity is replaced by the necessity for boundless economic development, the satisfaction of primary human needs is replaced by an uninterrupted fabrication of pseudo-needs which are reduced to the single pseudo-need of maintaining the reign of the autonomous economy. The autonomous economy permanently breaks away from fundamental need to the extent that it emerges from the *social unconscious* which unknowingly depended on it. "All that is conscious wears out. What is unconscious remains unalterable. But once freed, does it not fall to ruins in turn?" (Freud).

52

As soon as society discovers that it depends on the economy, the economy, in fact, depends on society. This subterranean force, which grew until it appeared sovereign, has lost its power. That which was the economic *it* must become the *I*. The subject can emerge only from society, namely from the struggle within society. The subject's possible existence depends on the outcome of the class struggle which shows itself to be the product and the producer of the economic foundation of history.

53

The consciousness of desire and the desire for consciousness are identically the project which, in its negative form, seeks the abolition of classes, the workers' direct possession of every aspect of their activity. Its *opposite* is the society of the spectacle, where the commodity contemplates itself in a world it has created.

III

Unity and Division within Appearance

A lively, new polemic about the concepts "one divides into two" and "two fuse into one" is unfolding on the philosophical front in the country. This debate is a struggle between those who are for and those who are against the materialist dialectic, a struggle between two conceptions of the world: the proletarian and the bourgeois conception. Those who maintain that "one divides into two" is the fundamental law of things are on the side of the materialist dialectic; those who maintain that the fundamental law of things is that "two fuse into one" are against the materialist dialectic. The two sides have drawn a clear line of demarcation between them, and their arguments are diametrically opposed. This polemic reflects, on the ideological level, the acute and complex class struggle taking place in China and in the world.

—*The Red Flag of Peking*, September 21, 1964

The spectacle, like modern society, is at once unified and divided. Like society, it builds its unity on the disjunction. But the contradiction, when it emerges in the spectacle, is in turn contradicted by a reversal of its meaning, so that the demonstrated division is unitary, while the demonstrated unity is divided.

The struggle of powers constituted for the management of the same socio-economic system is disseminated as the official contradiction but is in fact part of the real unity—on a world scale as well as within every nation.

The spectacular sham struggles of rival forms of separate power are at the same time real in that they translate the unequal and antagonistic development of the system, the relatively contradictory interests of classes or subdivisions of classes which acknowledge the system and define themselves as participants within its power. Just as the development of the most advanced economy is a clash between some priorities and others, the totalitarian management of the economy by a State bureaucracy and the condition of the countries within the sphere of colonization or semi-colonization are defined by specific peculiarities in the varieties of production and power. These diverse oppositions can be passed off in the spectacle as absolutely distinct forms of society (by means of any number of different criteria). But in actual fact, the truth of the uniqueness of all these specific sectors resides in the universal system that contains them: the unique movement that makes the planet its field, capitalism.

The society which carries the spectacle does not dominate the underdeveloped regions by its economic hegemony alone. It dominates them as the society of the spectacle. Even where the material base is still absent, modern society has already invaded the social surface of each continent by means of the spectacle. It defines the program of the ruling class and presides over its formation. Just as it presents pseudo-goods to be coveted, it offers false models of revolution to local revolutionaries. The spectacle of bureaucratic power, which holds sway over some industrial countries, is an integral part of the total spectacle, its general pseudo-negation and support. The spectacle displays certain totalitarian specializations of communication and administration when viewed locally, but when viewed in terms of the functioning of the entire system these specializations merge in a *world division of spectacular tasks.*

58

The division of spectacular tasks preserves the entirety of the existing order and especially the dominant pole of its development. The root of the spectacle is within the abundant economy—the source of the fruits which ultimately take over the spectacular market despite the ideological-police protectionist barriers of local spectacles aspiring to autarchy.

59

Under the shimmering diversions of the spectacle, *banalization* dominates modern society the world over and at every point where the developed consumption of commodities has seemingly multiplied the roles and objects to choose from. The remains of religion and of the family (the principal relic of the heritage of class power) and the moral repression they assure, merge whenever the enjoyment of *this* world is affirmed—this world being nothing other than repressive pseudo-enjoyment. The smug acceptance of what exists can also merge with purely spectacular rebellion; this reflects the simple fact that dissatisfaction itself became a commodity as soon as economic abundance could extend production to the processing of such raw materials.

60

The celebrity, the spectacular representation of a living human being, embodies this banality by embodying the image of a possible role. Being a star means specializing in the *seemingly lived;* the star is the object of identification with the shallow seeming life that has to compensate for the fragmented productive specializations which are actually lived. Celebrities exist to act out various styles of living and viewing society —unfettered, free to express themselves *globally.* They embody the inaccessible result of social *labor* by dramatizing its by-products magically projected above it as its goal: *power and vacations,* decision and consumption, which are the beginning and end of an undiscussed process. In one case state power personalizes itself as a pseudo-star; in another a star of con-sumption gets elected as a pseudo-power over the lived. But just as the activities of the star are not really global, they are not really varied.

61

The agent of the spectacle placed on stage as a star is the opposite of the individual, the enemy of the individual in him-self as well as in others. Passing into the spectacle as a model for identification, the agent renounces all autonomous qualities in order to identify himself with the general law of obedience to the course of things. The consumption celebrity superficially represents different types of personality and shows each of these types having equal access to the totality of consumption and finding similar happiness there. The decision celebrity must possess a complete stock of accepted human qualities. Official differences between stars are wiped out by the official similarity which is the presupposition of their excellence in everything. Khrushchev became a general so as to make deci-sions on the battle of Kursk, not on the spot, but at the twen-tieth anniversary, when he was master of the State. Kennedy remained an orator even to the point of proclaiming the eulogy over his own tomb, since Theodore Sorenson continued to edit speeches for the successor in the style which had characterized the personality of the deceased. The admirable people in whom the system personifies itself are well known for not being what they are; they became great men by stooping below the reality of the smallest individual life, and everyone knows it.

62

False choice in spectacular abundance, a choice which lies in the juxtaposition of competing and complimentary spectacles and also in the juxtaposition of roles (signified and carried mainly by things) which are at once exclusive and overlapping, develops into a struggle of vaporous qualities meant to stimulate loyalty to quantitative triviality. This resurrects false archaic oppositions, regionalisms and racisms which serve to raise the vulgar hierarchic ranks of consumption to a preposterous ontological superiority. In this way, the endless series of trivial confrontations is set up again, from competitive sports to elections, mobilizing a sub-ludic interest. Wherever there is abundant consumption, a major spectacular opposition between youth and adults comes to the fore among the false roles—false because the adult, master of his life, does not exist and because youth, the transformation of what exists, is in no way the property of those who are now young, but of the economic system, of the dynamism of capitalism. *Things* rule and are young; things confront and replace one another.

63

What hides under the spectacular oppositions is a *unity of misery*. Behind the masks of total choice, different forms of the same alienation confront each other, all of them built on real contradictions which are repressed. The spectacle exists in a *concentrated* or a *diffuse* form depending on the necessities of the particular stage of misery which it denies and supports. In both cases, the spectacle is nothing more than an image of happy unification surrounded by desolation and fear at the tranquil center of misery.

64

The concentrated spectacle belongs essentially to bureaucratic capitalism, even though it may be imported as a technique of state power in mixed backward economies or, at certain moments of crisis, in advanced capitalism. In fact, bureaucratic property itself is concentrated in such a way that the individual bureaucrat relates to the ownership of the global economy only through an intermediary, the bureaucratic community, and only as a member of this community. Moreover, the production of commodities, less developed in bureaucratic capitalism, also takes on a concentrated form: the commodity the bureaucracy holds on to is the totality of social labor, and what it sells back to society is wholesale survival. The dictatorship of the bureaucratic economy cannot leave the exploited masses any significant margin of choice, since the bureaucracy itself has to choose everything and since any other external choice, whether it concern food or music, is already a choice to destroy the bureaucracy completely. This dictatorship must be accompanied by permanent violence. The imposed image of the good envelops in its spectacle the totality of what officially exists, and is usually concentrated in one man, who is the guarantee of totalitarian cohesion. Everyone must magically identify with this absolute celebrity—or disappear. This celebrity is master of non-consumption, and the heroic image which gives an acceptable meaning to the absolute exploitation that primitive accumulation accelerated by terror really is. If every Chinese must learn Mao, and thus be Mao, it is because *he can be nothing else.* Wherever the concentrated spectacle rules, so does the police.

65

The diffuse spectacle accompanies the abundance of commodities, the undisturbed development of modern capitalism. Here every individual commodity is justified in the name of the grandeur of the production of the totality of objects of which the spectacle is an apologetic catalogue. Irreconcilable claims crowd the stage of the affluent economy's unified spectacle; different star-commodities simultaneously support contradictory projects for provisioning society: the spectacle of automobiles demands a perfect transport network which destroys old cities, while the spectacle of the city itself requires museum-areas. Therefore the already problematic satisfaction which is supposed to come from the *consumption of the whole,* is falsified immediately since the actual consumer can directly touch only a succession of fragments of this commodity happiness, fragments in which the quality attributed to the whole is obviously missing every time.

66

Every given commodity fights for itself, cannot acknowledge the others, and attempts to impose itself everywhere as if it were the only one. The spectacle, then, is the epic poem of this struggle, an epic which cannot be concluded by the fall of any Troy. The spectacle does not sing the praises of men and their weapons, but of commodities and their passions. In this blind struggle every commodity, pursuing its passion, unconsciously realizes something higher: the becoming-world of the commodity, which is also the becoming-commodity of the world. Thus, by means of a *ruse of commodity logic,* what's *specific* in the commodity wears itself out in the fight while the commodity-form moves toward its absolute realization.

67

The satisfaction which no longer comes from the use of abundant commodities is now sought in the recognition of their value as commodities: the use *of commodities* becomes sufficient unto itself; the consumer is filled with religious fervor for the sovereign liberty of the commodities. Waves of enthusiasm for a given product, supported and spread by all the media of communication, are thus propagated with lightning speed. A style of dress emerges from a film; a magazine promotes night spots which launch various clothing fads. Just when the mass of commodities slides toward puerility, the purile itself becomes a special commodity; this is epitomized by the *gadget.* We can recognize a mystical abandon to the transcendence of the commodity in free gifts, such as key chains which are not bought but are included by advertisers with prestigious purchases, or which flow by exchange in their own sphere. One who collects the key chains which have been manufactured for collection, accumulates the *indulgences of the commodity,* a glorious sign of his real presence among the faithful. Reified man advertises the proof of his intimacy with the commodity. The fetishism of commodities reaches moments of fervent exaltation similar to the ecstasies of the convulsions and miracles of the old religious fetishism. The only use which remains here is the fundamental use of submission.

68

The pseudo-need imposed by modern consumption clearly cannot be opposed by any genuine need or desire which is not itself shaped by society and its history. The abundant commodity stands for the total breach in the organic development of social needs. Its mechanical accumulation liberates *unlimited artificiality,* in the face of which living desire is helpless. The cumulative power of independent artificiality sows everywhere the *falsification of social life.*

In the image of the society happily unified by consumption, real division is only *suspended* until the next non-accomplishment in consumption. Every single product represents the hope for a dazzling shortcut to the promised land of total consumption and is ceremoniously presented as the decisive entity. But as with the diffusion of seemingly aristocratic first names carried by almost all individuals of the same age, the objects which promise unique powers can be recommended to the devotion of the masses only if they're produced in quantities large enough for mass consumption. A product acquires prestige when it is placed at the center of social life as the revealed mystery of the ultimate goal of production. But the object which was prestigious in the spectacle becomes vulgar as soon as it is taken home by its consumer—and by all its other consumers. It reveals its essential poverty (which naturally comes to it from the misery of its production) too late. But by then another object already carries the justification of the system and demands to be acknowledged.

70

The fraud of satisfaction exposes itself by being replaced, by following the change of products and of the general conditions of production. That which asserted its definitive excellence with perfect impudence nevertheless changes, both in the diffuse and the concentrated spectacle, and it is the system alone which must continue: Stalin as well as the outmoded commodity are denounced precisely by those who imposed them. Every *new lie* of advertising is also an *avowal* of the previous lie. The fall of every figure with totalitarian power reveals the *illusory community* which had approved him unanimously, and which had been nothing more than an agglomeration of solitudes without illusions.

71

What the spectacle offers as eternal is based on change and must change with its base. The spectacle is absolutely dogmatic and at the same time cannot really achieve any solid dogma. Nothing stops for the spectacle; this condition is natural to it, yet completely opposed to its inclination.

The unreal unity proclaimed by the spectacle masks the class division on which the real unity of the capitalist mode of production rests. What obliges the producers to participate in the construction of the world is also what separates them from it. What brings together men liberated from their local and national boundaries is also what pulls them apart. What requires a more profound rationality is also what nourishes the irrationality of hierarchic exploitation and repression. What creates the abstract power of society creates its concrete *unfreedom.*

IV

The Proletariat as Subject and as Representation

The equal right of all to the goods and joys of this world, the destruction of all authority, the negation of all moral restraint—there, if one goes to the heart of the matter, is the reason for the insurrection of March 18th and the charter of the formidable association which furnished it with an army.

—*Parliamentary Inquest on the Insurrection of March 18th*

The real movement which suppresses existing conditions rules over society from the moment of the bourgeoisie's victory in the economy, and visibly after the political translation of this victory. The development of productive forces shatters the old relations of production and all static order turns to dust. Whatever was absolute becomes historical.

By being thrown into history, by having to participate in the labor and struggles which make up history, men find themselves obliged to view their relations in a clear manner. This history has no object distinct from what takes place within it, even though the last unconscious metaphysical vision of the historical epoch could look at the productive progression through which history has unfolded as the very object of history. The *subject* of history can be none other than the living producing himself, becoming master and possessor of his world which is history, and existing as *consciousness of his game.*

The class struggles of the long *revolutionary epoch* inaugurated by the rise of the bourgeoisie, develop together with *the thought of history,* the dialectic, the thought which no longer stops to look for the meaning of what is, but rises to a knowledge of the dissolution of all that is, and in its movement dissolves all separation.

Hegel no longer had to *interpret* the world, but the *transformation* of the world. By *only interpreting* the transformation, Hegel is only the *philosophical* completion of philosophy. He wants to understand a world *which makes itself.* This historical thought is as yet only the consciousness which always arrives too late, and which pronounces the justification after the fact. Thus it has gone beyond separation only *in thought.* The paradox which consists of making the meaning of all reality depend on its historical completion, and at the same time of revealing this meaning as it makes itself the completion of history, flows from the simple fact that the thinker of the bourgeois revolutions of the 17th and 18th centuries sought in his philosophy only a *reconciliation* with the results of these revolutions. "Even as a philosophy of the bourgeois revolution, it does not express the entire process of this revolution, but only its final conclusion. In this sense, it is not a philosophy of the revolution, but of the restoration" (Karl Korsch, *Theses on Hegel and Revolution*). Hegel did, for the last time, the work of the philosopher, "the glorification of what exists"; but what existed for him could already be nothing less than the totality of historical movement. The *external* position of thought having in fact been preserved, it could be masked only by the identification of thought with an earlier project of Spirit, absolute hero who did what he wanted and wanted what he did, and whose accomplishment coincides with the present. Thus philosophy, which dies in the thought of history, can now glorify its world only by renouncing it, since in order to speak, it must presuppose that this total history to which it has reduced everything is already complete, and that the only tribunal where the judgment of truth could be given is closed.

77

When the proletariat demonstrates by its own existence, through acts, that this thought of history is not forgotten, the exposure of the *conclusion* is at the same time the confirmation of the method.

78

The thought of history can be saved only by becoming practical thought; and the practice of the proletariat as a revolutionary class cannot be less than historical consciousness operating on the totality of its world. All the theoretical currents of the *revolutionary* workers' movement grew out of a critical confrontation with Hegelian thought—Stirner and Bakunin as well as Marx.

79

The inseparability of Marx's theory from the Hegelian method is itself inseparable from the revolutionary character of this theory, namely from its truth. This first relationship has been generally ignored, misunderstood, and even denounced as the weakness of what fallaciously became a marxist *doctrine*. Bernstein, in his *Evolutionary Socialism: A Criticism and Affirmation (Die Voraussetzungen des Sozialismus und die Aufgaben der Sozialdemokratie)*, perfectly reveals the connection between the dialectical method and historical *partisanship*, by deploring the unscientific forecasts of the 1847 *Manifesto* on the imminence of proletarian revolution in Germany: "This historical self-deception, so erroneous that any political visionary could hardly have improved on it, would be incomprehensible in a Marx, who at that time had already seriously studied economics, if we did not see in this the product of a relic of the antithetical Hegelian dialectic from which Marx, no less than Engels, could never completely free himself. In those times of general effervescence, this was all the more fatal to him."

80

The *inversion* carried out by Marx to "recover through transfer" the thought of the bourgeois revolutions does not trivially consist of putting the materialist development of productive forces in the place of the journey of the Hegelian Spirit moving towards its encounter with itself in time, its objectification being identical to its alienation, and its historical wounds leaving no scars. History become real no longer has an *end*. Marx ruined Hegel's position as *separate* from what happens, as well as *contemplation* by any supreme external agent whatever. From now on, theory has to know only what it does. As opposed to this, contemplation of the economy's movement within the dominant thought of the present society is the *untranscended* heritage of the *undialectical* part of Hegel's search for a circular system: it is an approval which has lost the dimension of the concept and which no longer needs a Hegelianism to justify itself, because the movement which it praises is no more than a sector without a world view, a sector whose mechanical development effectively dominates the whole. Marx's project is the project of a conscious history. The quantitative which arises in the blind development of merely economic productive forces must be transformed into a qualitative historical appropriation. The *critique of political economy* is the first act of this *end of prehistory*: "Of all the instruments of production the greatest productive power is the revolutionary class itself."

What closely links Marx's theory with scientific thought is the rational understanding of the forces which really operate in society. But Marx's theory is fundamentally beyond scientific thought, and it preserves scientific thought only by superseding it: what is in question is an understanding of *struggle*, and not of *law*. "We know only one science: the science of history" (*The German Ideology*).

The bourgeois epoch, which wants to give a scientific foundation to history, overlooks the fact that this available science needed a historical foundation along with the economy. Inversely, history directly depends on economic knowledge only to the extent that it remains *economic history*. The extent to which the viewpoint of scientific observation could overlook the role of history in the economy (the global process which modifies its own basic scientific premises) is shown by the vanity of those socialist calculations which thought they had established the exact periodicity of crises. Now that the constant intervention of the State has succeeded in compensating for the effect of tendencies toward crisis, the same type of reasoning sees in this equilibrium a definitive economic harmony. The project of mastering the economy, the project of appropriating history, if it must know—and absorb—the science of society, cannot itself be *scientific*. The revolutionary viewpoint of a movement which thinks it can dominate current history by means of scientific knowledge remains *bourgeois*.

The utopian currents of socialism, although themselves historically grounded in the critique of the existing social organization, can rightly be called utopian to the extent that they reject history—namely the real struggle taking place, as well as the passage of time beyond the immutable perfection of their picture of a happy society—but not because they reject science. On the contrary, the utopian thinkers are completely dominated by the scientific thought of earlier centuries. They sought the completion of this general rational system: they did not in any way consider themselves disarmed prophets, since they believed in the social power of scientific proof and even, in the case of Saint-Simonism, in the seizure of power by science. "How did they want to seize through struggle what must be *proved?*" asked Sombart. The scientific conception of the uto-pians did not extend to the knowledge that some social groups have interests in the existing situation, forces to maintain it, and also forms of false consciousness corresponding to such positions. This conception did not even reach the historical reality of the development of science itself, which was oriented largely by the *social demand* of agents who selected not only what could be admitted, but also what could be studied. The utopian socialists, remaining prisoners of the *mode of exposition of scientific truth,* conceived this truth in terms of its pure abstract image—an image which had been imposed at a much earlier stage of society. As Sorel observed, it is on the model of *astronomy* that the utopians thought they would discover and demonstrate the laws of society. The harmony envisaged by them, hostile to history, grows out of the attempt to apply to society the science least dependent on history. This harmony is introduced with the experimental innocence of Newtonianism, and the happy destiny which is constantly postulated "plays in their social science a role analogous to the role of inertia in rational mechanics" *(Materiaux pour une théorie du prolétariat).*

84

The deterministic-scientific facet in Marx's thought was precisely the gap through which the process of "ideologiza-tion" penetrated, during his own lifetime, into the theoretical heritage left to the workers' movement. The arrival of the his-torical subject continues to be postponed, and it is economics, the historical science par excellence, which tends increasingly to guarantee the necessity of its own future negation. But what is pushed out of the field of theoretical vision in this manner is revolutionary practice, the only truth of this negation. What becomes important is to study economic development with patience, and to continue to accept suffering with a Hegelian tranquility, so that the result remains "a graveyard of good intentions." It is suddenly discovered that, according to the science of revolution, *consciousness always comes too soon,* and has to be taught. "History has shown that we, and all who thought as we did, were wrong. History has clearly shown that the state of economic development on the continent at that time was far from being ripe. . . ," Engels was to say in 1895. Throughout his life, Marx had maintained a unitary point of view in his theory, but the *exposition* of the theory was carried out on the *terrain* of the dominant thought and became precise in the form of critiques of particular disciplines, principally the critique of the fundamental science of bourgeois society, political economy. It is this mutilation, later accepted as definitive, which has constituted "marxism."

85

The weakness of Marx's theory is naturally the weakness of the revolutionary struggle of the proletariat of his time. The working class did not set off the permanent revolution in the Germany of 1848; the Commune was defeated in isolation. Revolutionary theory thus could not yet achieve its own total existence. The fact that Marx was reduced to defending and clarifying it with cloistered, scholarly work, in the British Museum, caused a loss in the theory itself. The scientific justifications Marx elaborated about the future development of the working class and the organizational practice that went with them became obstacles to proletarian consciousness at a later stage.

86

All the theoretical insufficiencies of content as well as form of exposition of the *scientific* defense of proletarian revolution can be traced to the identification of the proletariat with the bourgeoisie *from the standpoint of the revolutionary seizure of power.*

87

By grounding the proof of the scientific validity of proletarian power on *repeated* past attempts, Marx obscured his historical thought, from the *Manifesto* on, and was forced to support a *linear* image of the development of modes of production brought on by class struggles which end, each time, "with a revolutionary transformation of the entire society or with mutual destruction of the classes in struggle." But in the observable reality of history, as Marx pointed out elsewhere, the "Asiatic mode of production" preserved its immobility in spite of all class confrontations, just as the serf uprisings never defeated the landlords, nor the slave revolts of Antiquity the free men. The linear schema loses sight of the fact that *the bourgeoisie is the only revolutionary class that ever won;* at the same time it is the only class for which the development of the economy was the cause and the consequence of its taking hold of society. The same simplification led Marx to neglect the economic role of the State in the management of a class society. If the rising bourgeoisie seemed to liberate the economy from the State, this took place only to the extent that the former State was an instrument of class oppression in a *static economy.* The bourgeoisie developed its autonomous economic power in the medieval period of the weakening of the State, at the moment of feudal fragmentation of balanced powers. But the modern State which, through Mercantilism, began to support the development of the bourgeoisie, and which finally became *its State* at the time of "laisser faire, laisser passer," was to reveal later that it was endowed with the central power of calculated management of the *economic process.* With the concept of *Bonapartism,* Marx was nevertheless able to describe the shape of the modern statist bureaucracy, the fusion of capital and State, the formation of a "national power of capital over labor, a public force organized for social enslavement," where the bourgeoisie renounces all historical life which is not reduced to the economic history of things and would like to "be condemned to the same political nothingness as other classes." Here the socio-political foundations of the modern spectacle are already established, negatively defining the proletariat as *the only pretender to historical life.*

88

The only two classes which effectively correspond to Marx's theory, the two pure classes towards which the entire analysis of *Capital* leads, the bourgeoisie and the proletariat, are also the only two revolutionary classes in history, but in very different conditions: the bourgeois revolution is over; the proletarian revolution is a project born on the foundation of the preceding revolution but differing from it qualitatively. By neglecting the *originality* of the historical role of the bourgeoisie, one masks the concrete originality of the proletarian project, which can attain nothing unless it carries its own banners and knows the "immensity of its tasks." The bourgeoisie came to power because it is the class of the developing economy. The proletariat cannot itself come to power except by becoming the *class of consciousness.* The growth of productive forces cannot guarantee such power, even by way of the increasing dispossession which it brings about. A Jacobin seizure of power cannot be its instrument. No *ideology* can help the proletariat disguise its partial goals as general goals, because the proletariat cannot preserve any partial reality which is really its own.

89

If Marx, in a given period of his participation in the struggle of the proletariat, expected too much from scientific forecasting, to the point of creating the intellectual foundation for the illusions of economism, it is known that he did not personally succumb to those illusions. In a well-known letter of December 7, 1867, accompanying an article where he himself criticized *Capital,* an article which Engels would later present to the press as the work of an adversary, Marx clearly disclosed the limits of his own science: " . . . The *subjective* tendency of the author (which was perhaps imposed on him by his political position and his past), namely the manner in which he views and presents to others the ultimate results of the real movement, the real social process, has no relation to his own actual analysis." Thus Marx, by denouncing the "tendentious conclusions" of his own objective analysis, and by the irony of the "perhaps" with reference to the extra-scientific choices imposed on him, at the same time shows the methodological key to the fusion of the two aspects.

90

The fusion of knowledge and action must be realized in the historical struggle itself, in such a way that each of these terms guarantees the truth of the other. The formation of the proletarian class into a subject means the organization of revolutionary struggles and the organization of society at the *revolutionary moment:* it is then that the *practical conditions of consciousness* must exist, conditions in which the theory of praxis is confirmed by becoming practical theory. However, this central question of organization was the question least developed by revolutionary theory at the time when the workers' movement was founded, namely when this theory still had the *unitary* character which came from the thought of history. (Theory had undertaken precisely this task in order to develop a unitary historical *practice.*) This question is in fact the locus of *inconsistency* of this theory, allowing the return of statist and hierarchic methods of application borrowed from the bourgeois revolution. The forms of organization of the workers' movement which were developed on the basis of this renunciation of theory have in turn prevented the maintenance of a unitary theory, breaking it up into varied specialized and partial disciplines. Due to the betrayal of unitary historical thought, this ideological estrangement from theory can no longer recognize the practical verification of this thought when such verification emerges in spontaneous struggles of workers; all it can do is repress every manifestation and memory of such verification. Yet these historical forms which appeared in struggle are precisely the practical milieu which the theory needed in order to be true. They are requirements of the theory which have not been formulated theoretically. The *soviet* was not a theoretical discovery; yet its existence in practice was already the highest theoretical truth of the International Workingmen's Association.

91

The first successes of the struggle of the International led it to free itself from the confused influences of the dominant ideology which survived in it. But the defeat and repression which it soon encountered brought to the foreground a conflict between two conceptions of the proletarian revolution. Both of these conceptions contain an *authoritarian* dimension and thus abandon the conscious self-emancipation of the working class. In effect, the quarrel between Marxists and Bakuninists (which became irreconcilable) was two-edged, referring at once to power in the revolutionary society and to the organization of the present movement, and when the positions of the adversaries passed from one aspect to the other, they reversed themselves. Bakunin fought the illusion of abolishing classes by the authoritarian use of state power, foreseeing the reconstitution of a dominant bureaucratic class and the dictatorship of the most knowledgeable, or those who would be reputed to be such. Marx thought that the growth of economic contradictions inseparable from democratic education of the workers would reduce the role of the proletarian State to a simple phase of legalizing the new social relations imposing themselves objectively, and denounced Bakunin and his followers for the authoritarianism of a conspiratorial elite which deliberately placed itself above the International and formulated the extravagant design of imposing on society the irresponsible dictatorship of those who are most revolutionary, or those who would designate themselves to be such. Bakunin, in fact, recruited followers on the basis of such a perspective: "Invisible pilots in the center of the popular storm, we must direct it, not with a visible power, but with the collective dictatorship of all the *allies*. A dictatorship without badge, without title, without official right, yet all the more powerful because it will have none of the appearances of power." Thus two *ideologies* of the workers' revolution opposed each other, each containing a partially true critique, but losing the unity of the thought of history, and instituting themselves into ideological *authorities*. Powerful organizations, like German Social-Democracy and the Iberian Anarchist Federation faithfully served one or the other of these ideologies; and everywhere the result was very different from what had been desired.

92

The strength and the weakness of the real anarchist struggle resides in its viewing the goal of proletarian revolution as *immediately present* (the pretensions of anarchism in its individualist variants have always been laughable). From the historical thought of modern class struggles collectivist anarchism retains only the conclusion, and its exclusive insistence on this conclusion is accompanied by deliberate contempt for method. Thus its critique of the *political struggle* has remained abstract, while its choice of economic struggle is affirmed only as a function of the illusion of a definitive solution brought about by one single blow on this terrain—on the day of the general strike or the insurrection. The anarchists *have an ideal to realize*. Anarchism remains a *merely ideological* negation of the State and of classes, namely of the social conditions of separate ideology. It is the *ideology of pure liberty* which equalizes everything and dismisses the very idea of historical evil. This viewpoint which fuses all partial desires has given anarchism the merit of representing the rejection of existing conditions in favor of the whole of life, and not of a privileged critical specialization; but this fusion is considered in the absolute, according to individual caprice, before its actual realization, thus condemning anarchism to an incoherence too easily seen through. Anarchism has merely to repeat and to replay the same simple, total conclusion in every single struggle, because this first conclusion was from the beginning identified with the entire outcome of the movement. Thus Bakunin could write in 1873, when he left the Fédération Jurassiene: "During the past nine years, more ideas have been developed within the International than would be needed to save the world, if ideas alone could save it, and I challenge anyone to invent a new one. It is no longer the time for ideas, but for facts and acts." There is no doubt that this conception retains an element of the historical thought of the proletariat, the certainty that ideas must become practice, but it leaves the historical terrain by assuming that the adequate forms for this passage to practice have already been found and will never change.

93

The anarchists, who distinguish themselves explicitly from the rest of the workers' movement by their ideological conviction, reproduce this separation of competences among themselves; they provide a terrain favorable to informal domination over all anarchist organizations by propagandists and defenders of their ideology, specialists who are in general more mediocre the more their intellectual activity consists of the repetition of certain definitive truths. Ideological respect for unanimity of decision has on the whole been favorable to the uncontrolled authority, within the organization itself, of *specialists in freedom;* and revolutionary anarchism expects the same type of unanimity from the liberated population, obtained by the same means. Furthermore, the refusal to take into account the opposition between the conditions of a minority grouped in the present struggle and of a society of free individuals, has nourished a permanent separation among anarchists at the moment of common decision, as is shown by an infinity of anarchist insurrections in Spain, confined and destroyed on a local level.

94

The illusion entertained more or less explicitly by genuine anarchism is the permanent imminence of an instantaneously accomplished revolution which will prove the truth of the ideology and of the mode of practical organization derived from the ideology. In 1936, anarchism in fact led a social revolution, the most advanced model of proletarian power in all time. In this context it should be noted that the signal for a general insurrection had been imposed by a *pronunciamiento* of the army. Furthermore, to the extent that this revolution was not completed during the first days (because of the existence of Franco's power in half the country, strongly supported from abroad while the rest of the international proletarian movement was already defeated, and because of remains of bourgeois forces or other statist workers' parties within the camp of the Republic) the organized anarchist movement showed itself unable to extend the demi-victories of the revolution, or even to defend them. Its known leaders became ministers and hostages of the bourgeois State which destroyed the revolution only to lose the civil war.

95

The "orthodox Marxism" of the Second International is the scientific ideology of the socialist revolution: it identifies its whole truth with objective processes in the economy and with the progress of a recognition of this necessity by the working class educated by the organization. This ideology rediscovers the confidence in pedagogical demonstration which had characterized utopian socialism, but mixes it with a *contemplative* reference to the course of history: this attitude has lost as much of the Hegelian dimension of a total history as it has lost the immobile image of totality in the utopian critique (most highly developed by Fourier). This scientific attitude can do no more than revive a symmetry of ethical choices; it is from this attitude that the nonsense of Hilferding springs when he states that recognizing the necessity of socialism gives "no indication of the practical attitude to be adopted. For it is one thing to recognize a necessity, and it is quite another thing to put oneself at the service of this necessity" (*Finanzkapital*). Those who failed to recognize that for Marx and for the revolutionary proletariat the unitary thought of history *was in no way distinct from the practical attitude to be adopted*, regularly became victims of the practice they adopted.

96

The ideology of the social-democratic organization gave power to *professors* who educated the working class, and the form of organization which was adopted was the form most suitable for this passive apprenticeship. The participation of socialists of the Second International in political and economic struggles was admittedly concrete but profoundly *uncritical*. It was conducted in the name of *revolutionary illusion* by means of an obviously *reformist* practice. The revolutionary ideology was to be shattered by the very success of those who held it.

The separate position of the movement's deputies and journalists attracted the already recruited bourgeois intellectuals toward a bourgeois mode of life. Even those who had been recruited from the struggles of industrial workers and who were themselves workers, were transformed by the union bureaucracy into brokers of labor power who sold labor as a commodity, for a just price. If their activity was to retain some appearance of being revolutionary, capitalism would have had to be conveniently unable to support economically this reformism which it tolerated politically (in the legalistic agitation of the social-democrats). But such an antagonism, guaranteed by their science, was constantly belied by history.

97

Bernstein, the social-democrat furthest from political ideology and most openly attached to the methodology of bourgeois science, had the honesty to want to demonstrate the reality of this contradiction; the English workers' reformist movement had also demonstrated it, by doing without revolutionary ideology. But the contradiction was definitively demonstrated only by historical development itself. Although full of illusions in other respects, Bernstein had denied that a crisis of capitalist production would miraculously force the hand of socialists who wanted to inherit the revolution only by this legitimate rite. The profound social upheaval which arose with the first world war, though fertile with the awakening of consciousness, twice demonstrated that the social-democratic hierarchy had not educated revolutionarily; and had in no way transformed the German workers into *theoreticians*: first when the vast majority of the party rallied to the imperialist war; next when, in defeat, it squashed the Spartakist revolutionaries. The ex-worker Ebert still believed in sin, since he admitted that he hated revolution "like sin." The same leader showed himself a precursor of the *socialist representation* which soon after confronted the Russian proletariat as its absolute enemy; he even formulated exactly the same program for this new alienation: "Socialism means working a lot."

98

Lenin, as a Marxist thinker, was no more than a consistent and *faithful Kautskyist* who applied the *revolutionary ideology* of "orthodox Marxism" to Russian conditions, conditions unfavorable to the reformist practice carried on elsewhere by the Second International. In the Russian context, the *external* management of the proletariat, acting by means of a disciplined clandestine party subordinated to intellectuals transformed into "professional revolutionaries," becomes a profession which refuses to deal with the ruling professions of capitalist society (the Czarist political regime being in any case unable to offer such opportunities, which are based on an advanced stage of bourgeois power). It therefore became the *profession of the absolute management* of society.

99

With the war and the collapse of the social-democratic international in the face of the war, the authoritarian ideological radicalism of the Bolsheviks spread all over the world. The bloody end of the democratic illusions of the workers' movement transformed the entire world into a Russia, and Bolshevism, reigning over the first revolutionary breach brought on by this epoch of crisis, offered to proletarians of all lands its hierarchic and ideological model, so that they could "speak Russian" to the ruling class. Lenin did not reproach the Marxism of the Second International for being a revolutionary *ideology*, but for ceasing to be one.

100

The historical moment when Bolshevism triumphed *for itself* in Russia and when social-democracy fought victoriously *for the old world* marks the inauguration of the state of affairs which is at the heart of the domination of the modern spectacle: the *representation of the working class* radically opposes itself to the working class.

101

"In all previous revolutions," wrote Rosa Luxemburg in *Rote Fahne* of December 21, 1918, "the combatants faced each other directly: class against class, program against program. In the present revolution, the troops protecting the old order do not intervene under the insignia of the ruling class, but under the flag of a 'social-democratic party.' If the central question of revolution had been posed openly and honestly: capitalism or socialism?—the great mass of the proletariat would today have no doubts or hesitations." Thus, a few days before its destruction, the radical current of the German proletariat discovered the secret of the new conditions which had been created by the preceding process (toward which the representation of the working class had greatly contributed): the spectacular organization of defense of the existing order, the social reign of appearances where no "central question" can any longer be posed "openly and honestly." The revolutionary representation of the proletariat had at this stage become both the main factor and the central result of the general falsification of society.

102

The organization of the proletariat on the Bolshevik model which emerged from Russian backwardness and from the abandonment of revolutionary struggle by the workers' movement of advanced countries, found in this backwardness all the conditions which carried this form of organization toward the counter-revolutionary inversion which it unconsciously contained at its source. The continuing retreat of the mass of the European workers' movement in the face of the *Hic Rhodus, hic salta* of the 1918-1920 period, a retreat which included the violent destruction of its radical minority, favored the completion of the Bolshevik development and let this fraudulent outcome present itself to the world as the only proletarian solution. By seizing state monopoly over representation and defense of workers' power, the Bolshevik party justified itself and *became what it was*: the party of the *proprietors of the proletariat* (essentially eliminating earlier forms of property).

103

During twenty years of unresolved theoretical debate, the varied tendencies of Russian social-democracy had examined all the conditions for the liquidation of Czarism: the weakness of the bourgeoisie, the weight of the peasant majority and the decisive role of a concentrated and combative but hardly numerous proletariat. The debate was resolved in practice by means of a factor which had not been present in the hypotheses: a revolutionary bureaucracy which directed the proletariat seized State power and gave society a new class domination. Strictly bourgeois revolution had been impossible; the "democratic dictatorship of workers and peasants" was meaningless; the proletarian power of the Soviets could not maintain itself simultaneously against the class of small landowners, against the national and international White reaction, and against its own representation externalized and alienated in the form of a workers' party of absolute masters of State, economy, expression, and soon of thought. The theory of permanent revolution of Trotsky and Parvus, which Lenin adopted in April 1917, was the only theory which became true for countries where the social development of the bourgeoisie was retarded, but this theory became true only after the introduction of the unknown factor: the class power of the bureaucracy. In the numerous arguments among the Bolshevik directors, Lenin was the most consistent defender of the concentration of dictatorial power in the hands of the supreme representatives of ideology. Lenin was right every time against his adversaries in that he supported the solution implied by earlier choices of absolute minority power: the democracy which was kept from peasants *by means of the state* would have to be kept from workers as well, which led to keeping it from communist leaders of unions, from the entire party, and finally from leading party bureaucrats. At the Tenth Congress, when the Kronstadt Soviet had been defeated by arms and buried under calumny, Lenin pronounced against the leftist bureaucrats of the "Workers' Opposition" the following conclusion (the logic of which Stalin later extended to a complete division of the world): "Here or there with a rifle, but not with opposition. . . We've had enough opposition."

104

After Kronstadt, the bureaucracy—sole proprietor of a *State Capitalism*—consolidated its power internally by means of a temporary alliance with the peasantry (with the "new economic policy") and externally by using workers regimented into the bureaucratic parties of the Third International as supports for Russian diplomacy, thus sabotaging the entire revolutionary movement and supporting bourgeois governments whose aid it needed in international politics (the power of the Kuomintang in China in 1925-27, the Popular Front in Spain and in France, etc.). The bureaucratic society continued the consolidation by terrorizing the peasantry in order to implement the most brutal primitive capitalist accumulation in history. The industrialization of the Stalin epoch revealed the reality behind the *bureaucracy:* the continuation of the power of the economy and the preservation of the essence of the market society—commodity labor. The independent economy, which dominates society to the extent of reinstituting the class domination it needs for its own ends, is thus confirmed. Which is to say that the bourgeoisie created an autonomous power which, so long as its autonomy lasts, can even do without a bourgeoisie. The totalitarian bureaucracy is not "the last owning class in history" in the sense of Bruno Rizzi; it is only a *substitute ruling class* for the commodity economy. Capitalist private property in decline is replaced by a simplified, less diversified surrogate which is condensed as collective property of the bureaucratic class. This underdeveloped ruling class is the expression of economic underdevelopment, and has no perspective other than to overcome the retardation of this development in certain regions of the world. It was the workers' party organized according to the bourgeois model of separation which furnished the hierarchical-statist cadre for this supplementary edition of a ruling class. While in one of Stalin's prisons, Anton Ciliga observed that "technical questions of organization turned out to be social questions" *(Lenin and the Revolution).*

105

Revolutionary ideology, the *coherence of the separate,* of which Leninism represents the greatest voluntaristic attempt, supervising a reality which rejects it, with Stalinism *returns to its truth in incoherence.* At that point ideology is no longer a weapon, but a goal. The lie which is no longer challenged becomes lunacy. Reality as well as the goal dissolve in the totalitarian ideological proclamation: all it says is all there is. This is a local primitivism of the spectacle, whose role is nevertheless essential in the development of the world spectacle. The ideology which is materialized in this context has not economically transformed the world, as has capitalism which reached the stage of abundance; it has merely transformed *perception* by means of the police.

106

The totalitarian-ideological class in power is the power of a topsy-turvy world: the stronger it is, the more it claims not to exist, and its force serves above all to affirm its nonexistence. It is modest only on this point, because its official nonexistence must also coincide with the *nec plus ultra* of historical development which must at the same time be attributed to its infallible command. Extended everywhere, the bureaucracy must be the *class invisible* to consciousness; as a result all social life becomes insane. The social organization of the absolute lie flows from this fundamental contradiction.

Stalinism was the reign of terror within the bureaucratic class itself. The terrorism at the base of this class's power must also strike this class because it possesses no juridical guarantee, no recognized existence as owning class, which it could extend to every one of its members. Its real property being hidden, the bureaucracy became proprietor by way of false consciousness. False consciousness can maintain its absolute power only by means of absolute terror, where all real motives are ultimately lost. The members of the bureaucratic class in power have a right of ownership over society only collectively, as participants in a fundamental lie: they have to play the role of the proletariat directing a socialist society; they have to be actors loyal to a script of ideological disloyalty. But effective participation in this falsehood requires that it be recognized as actual participation. No bureaucrat can support his right to power individually, since proving that he's a socialist proletarian would mean presenting himself as the opposite of a bureaucrat, and proving that he's a bureaucrat is impossible since the official truth of the bureaucracy is that it does not exist. Thus every bureaucrat depends absolutely on the *central guarantee* of the ideology which recognizes the collective participation in its "socialist power" of *all the bureaucrats it does not annihilate*. If all the bureaucrats taken together decide everything, the cohesion of their own class can be assured only by the concentration of their terrorist power in a single person. In this person resides the only practical truth of falsehood *in power*: the indisputable permanence of its constantly adjusted frontier. Stalin decides without appeal who is ultimately to be a possessing bureaucrat; in other words, who should be named "a proletarian in power" and who "a traitor in the pay of the Mikado or of Wall Street." The bureaucratic atoms find the common essence of their right only in the person of Stalin. Stalin is the world sovereign who in this manner knows himself as the absolute person for whose consciousness there is no higher spirit. "The sovereign of the world has effective consciousness of what he is—the universal power of efficacy—in the destructive violence which he exerts against the Self of his subjects, the contrasting others." Just as he is the power that defines the terrain of domination, he is *the power which ravages this terrain.*

108

When ideology, having become absolute through the possession of absolute power, changes from partial knowledge into totalitarian falsehood, the thought of history is so perfectly annihilated that history itself, even at the level of the most empirical knowledge, can no longer exist. The totalitarian bureaucratic society lives in a perpetual present where everything that happened exists for it only as a place accessible to its police. The project already formulated by Napoleon of "the ruler directing the energy of memory" has found its total concretization in a permanent manipulation of the past, not only of meanings but of facts as well. But the price paid for this emancipation from all historical reality is the loss of the rational reference which is indispensable to the *historical* society, capitalism. It is known how much the scientific application of insane ideology has cost the Russian economy, if only through the imposture of Lysenko. The contradiction of the totalitarian bureaucracy administering an industrialized society, caught between its need for rationality and its rejection of the rational, is one of its main deficiencies with regard to normal capitalist development. Just as the bureaucracy cannot resolve the question of agriculture the way capitalism had done, it is ultimately inferior to capitalism in industrial production, planned from the top and based on unreality and generalized falsehood.

109

Between the two world wars, the revolutionary workers' movement was annihilated by the joint action of the Stalinist bureaucracy and of fascist totalitarianism which had borrowed its form of organization from the totalitarian party tried out in Russia. Fascism was an extremist defense of the bourgeois economy threatened by crisis and by proletarian subversion. Fascism is a *state of siege* in capitalist society, by means of which this society saves itself and gives itself stop-gap rationalization by making the State intervene massively in its management. But this rationalization is itself burdened by the

immense irrationality of its means. Although fascism rallies to
the defense of the main points of bourgeois ideology which has
become conservative (the family, property, the moral order, the
nation), reuniting the petty-bourgeoisie and the unemployed
routed by crisis or deceived by the impotence of socialist revolution, it is not itself fundamentally ideological. It presents
itself as it is: a violent resurrection of *myth* which demands
participation in a community defined by archaic pseudo-
values: race, blood, the leader. Fascism is *technically-equipped
archaism*. Its decomposed *ersatz* of myth is revived in the spectacular context of the most modern means of conditioning and
illusion. Thus it is one of the factors in the formation of the
modern spectacle, and its role in the destruction of the old
workers' movement makes it one of the fundamental forces of
present-day society. However, since fascism is also *the most
costly* form of preserving the capitalist order, it usually had to
leave the front of the stage to the great roles played by the
capitalist States; it is eliminated by stronger and more rational
forms of the same order.

110

Now that the Russian bureaucracy has finally succeeded in
doing away with the remains of bourgeois property which
hampered its rule over the economy, in developing this property for its own use, and in being recognized externally among
the great powers, it wants to enjoy its world calmly and to
suppress the arbitrary element which had been exerted over it:
it denounces the Stalinism of its origin. But the denunciation
remains Stalinist, arbitrary, unexplained and continually cor-
rected, because *the ideological lie at its origin can never be
revealed*. Thus the bureaucracy can liberalize neither cultur-
ally nor politically because its existence as a class depends on
its ideological monopoly which, with all its weight, is its only
title to property. The ideology has no doubt lost the passion of
its positive affirmation, but the indifferent triviality which survives still has the repressive function of prohibiting the slight-
est competition, of holding captive the totality of thought.
Thus the bureaucracy is bound to an ideology which is no
longer believed by anyone. What used to be terrorist has become a laughing matter, but this laughing matter can maintain
itself only by preserving, as a last resort, the terrorism it would
like to be rid of. Thus precisely at the moment when the
bureaucracy wants to demonstrate its superiority on the terrain
of capitalism it reveals itself to be a *poor relation* of capitalism.
Just as its actual history contradicts its claims and its vulgarly

entertained ignorance contradicts its scientific pretentions, so its project of becoming a rival to the bourgeoisie in the production of commodity abundance is blocked by the fact that this abundance carries its *implicit ideology* within itself, and is usually accompanied by an indefinitely extended freedom of spectacular false choices, a pseudo-freedom which remains irreconcilable with the bureaucratic ideology.

111

At the present moment of its development, the bureaucracy's title to ideological property is already collapsing internationally. The power which established itself nationally as a fundamentally internationalist model must admit that it can no longer pretend to maintain its false cohesion over and above every national frontier. The unequal economic development of some bureaucracies with competing interests, who succeeded in acquiring their "socialism" beyond the single country, has led to the public and total confrontation between the Russian lie and the Chinese lie. From this point on, every bureaucracy in power, or every totalitarian party which is a candidate to the power left behind by the Stalinist period in some national working classes, must follow its own path. The global decomposition of the alliance of bureaucratic mystification is further aggravated by manifestations of internal negation which began to be visible to the world with the East Berlin

workers' revolt, opposing the bureaucrats with the demand for "a government of steel workers," manifestations which already once led all the way to the power of workers' councils in Hungary. However, the global decomposition of the bureaucratic alliance is in the last analysis the least favorable factor for the present development of capitalist society. The bourgeoisie is in the process of losing the adversary which objectively supported it by providing an illusory unification of all negation of the existing order. This division of labor within the spectacle comes to an end when the pseudo-revolutionary role in turn divides. The spectacular element of the collapse of the workers' movement will itself collapse.

112

The Leninist illusion has no contemporary base outside of the various Trotskyist tendencies. Here the identification of the proletarian project with a hierarchic organization of ideology stubbornly survives the experience of all its results. The distance which separates Trotskyism from a revolutionary critique of the present society allows Trotskyism to maintain a deferential attitude toward positions which were already false when they were used in a real combat. Trotsky remained basically in solidarity with the high bureaucracy until 1927, seeking to capture it so as to make it resume genuinely Bolshevik action externally (it is known that in order to conceal Lenin's famous

"testament" he went so far as to slanderously disavow his supporter Max Eastman, who had made it public). Trotsky was condemned by his basic perspective, because as soon as the bureaucracy recognizes itself in its result as a counter-revolutionary class internally, it must also choose, in the name of revolution, to be effectively counter-revolutionary externally, *just as it is at home.* Trotsky's subsequent struggle for the Fourth International contains the same inconsistency. All his life he refused to recognize the bureaucracy as the power of a separate class, because during the second Russian revolution he became an unconditional supporter of the Bolshevik form of organization. When Lukacs, in 1923, showed that this form was the long-sought mediation between theory and practice, in which the proletarians are no longer *"spectators"* of the events which happen in their organization, but consciously choose and live these events, he described as actual merits of the Bolshevik party everything that the Bolshevik party *was not.* Except for his profound theoretical work, Lukacs was still an ideologue speaking in the name of the power most grossly external to the proletarian movement, believing and making believe that he, himself, with his entire personality, was within this power as if it were *his own.* But the sequel showed just how this power disowns and suppresses its lackeys; in Lukacs' endless self-repudiations, just what he had identified with became visible and clear as a caricature: he had identified with the *opposite* of himself and of what he had supported in *History and Class Consciousness.* Lukacs is the best proof of the fundamental rule which judges all the intellectuals of this century: what they *respect* is an exact measure of their own *despicable* reality. Yet Lenin had hardly encouraged this type of illusion about his activity, considering that "a political party cannot examine its members to see if there are contradictions between their philosophy and the party program." The real party whose imaginary portrait Lukacs had inopportunely drawn was coherent for only one precise and partial task: to seize State power.

113

The neo-Leninist illusion of present-day Trotskyism, constantly exposed by the reality of modern bourgeois as well as bureaucratic capitalist societies, naturally finds a favored field of application in "underdeveloped" countries which are formally independent. Here the illusion of some variant of state and bureaucratic socialism is consciously manipulated by local ruling classes as *simply the ideology of economic development*. The hybrid composition of these classes is more or less clearly related to their standing along the bourgeois-bureaucratic spectrum. Their games on an international scale with the two poles of existing capitalist power, as well as their ideological compromises (notably with Islam), express the hybrid reality of their social base and remove from this final by-product of ideological socialism everything serious except the police. A bureaucracy establishes itself by staffing a national struggle and an agrarian peasant revolt; from that point on, as in China, it tends to apply the Stalinist model of industrialization in societies less developed than Russia was in 1917. A bureaucracy able to industrialize the nation can set itself up from among the petty-bourgeoisie, or out of army cadres who seize power, as in Egypt. A bureaucracy which sets itself up as a para-statist leadership during the struggle can, on certain questions, seek the equilibrium point of a compromise in order to fuse with a weak national bourgeoisie, as in Algeria at the beginning of its war of independence. Finally, in the former colonies of black Africa which remain openly tied to the American and European bourgeoisie, a bourgeoisie constitutes itself (usually on the basis of the power of traditional tribal chiefs) *by seizing the State*. These countries, where foreign imperialism remains the real master of the economy, enter a stage where the *compradores* have gotten an indigenous State as compensation for their sale of indigenous products, a State which is independent in the face of the local masses but not in the face of imperialism. This is an artificial bourgeoisie which is not able to accumulate, but which simply *squanders* the share of surplus value from local labor which reaches it as well as the foreign subsidies from the States or monopolies which protect it. Because of the obvious incapacity of these bourgeois classes to fulfill the normal economic function of a bourgeoisie, each of them faces a subversion based on the bureaucratic model, more or less adapted to local peculiarities, and eager to seize the heritage of this bourgeoisie. But the very success of a bureaucracy in its fundamental project of industrialization necessarily contains the perpsective of its historical defeat: by accumulating capital it accumulates a proletariat and thus creates its own negation in a country where it did not yet exist.

In this complex and terrible development which has carried the epoch of class struggles toward new conditions, the proletariat of the industrial countries has completely lost the affirmation of its autonomous perspective and also, in the last analysis, *its illusions*, but not its being. It has not been suppressed. It remains irreducibly in existence within the intensified alienation of modern capitalism: it is the immense majority of workers who have lost all power over the use of their lives and who, *once they know this*, redefine themselves as the proletariat, as negation at work within this society. The proletariat is objectively reinforced by the progressive disappearance of the peasantry and by the extension of the logic of factory labor to a large sector of "services" and intellectual professions. *Subjectively* the proletariat is still far removed from its practical class consciousness, not only among white collar workers but also among wage workers who have as yet discovered only the impotence and mystification of the old politics. Nevertheless, when the proletariat discovers that its own externalized power collaborates in the constant reinforcement of capitalist society, not only in the form of its labor but also in the form of unions, of parties, or of the state power it had built to emancipate itself, it also discovers from concrete historical experience that it is the class totally opposed to all congealed externalization and all specialization of power. It carries the *revolution which cannot let anything remain outside of itself*, the demand for the permanent domination of the present over the past, and the total critique of separation. It is this that must find its suitable form in action. No quantitative amelioration of its misery, no illusion of hierarchic integration is a lasting cure for its dissatisfaction, because the proletariat cannot truly recognize itself in a particular wrong it suffered nor in the righting of a *particular wrong*. It cannot recognize itself in the righting of a large number of wrongs either, but only in the *absolute wrong* of being relegated to the margin of life.

The new signs of negation multiplying in the economically developed countries, signs which are misunderstood and falsified by spectacular arrangement, already enable us to draw the conclusion that a new epoch has begun: now, after the workers' first attempt at subversion, *it is capitalist abundance which has failed*. When anti-union struggles of Western workers are repressed first of all by unions, and when the first amorphous protests launched by rebellious currents of youth directly imply the rejection of the old specialized politics, of art and of daily life, we see two sides of a new spontaneous struggle which begins under a *criminal* guise. These are the portents of a second proletarian assault against class society. When the lost children of this still immobile army reappear on this battleground which was altered and yet remains the same, they follow a new "General Ludd" who, this time, urges them to destroy the *machines of permitted consumption.*

116

"The political form at last discovered in which the economic emancipation of labor could be realized" has in this century acquired a clear outline in the revolutionary workers' Councils which concentrate in themselves all the functions of decision and execution, and federate with each other by means of delegates responsible to the base and revocable at any moment. Their actual existence has as yet been no more than a brief sketch, quickly opposed and defeated by various defensive forces of class society, among which their own false consciousness must often be included. Pannekoek rightly insisted that choosing the power of workers' Councils "poses problems" rather than providing a solution. Yet it is precisely in this power where the problems of the proletarian revolution can find their real solution. This is where the objective conditions of historical consciousness are reunited. This is where direct *active* communication is realized, where specialization, hierarchy and separation end, where the existing conditions have been transformed "into conditions of unity." Here the proletarian subject can emerge from his struggle against contemplation: his consciousness is equal to the practical organization which it undertakes because this consciousness is itself inseparable from coherent intervention in history.

117

In the power of the Councils, which must internationally supplant all other power, the proletarian movement is its own product and this product is the producer himself. He is to himself his own goal. Only there is the spectacular negation of life negated in its turn.

The appearance of the Councils was the highest reality of the proletarian movement in the first quarter of this century, a reality which was not seen or was travestied because it disappeared along with the rest of the movement that was negated and eliminated by the entire historical experience of the time. At the new moment of proletarian critique, this result returns as the only undefeated point of the defeated movement. Historical consciousness, which knows that this is the only milieu where it can exist, can now recognize this reality, no longer at the periphery of what is ebbing, but at the center of what is rising.

119

A revolutionary organization existing before the power of the Councils (it will find its own form through struggle), for all these historical reasons, already knows that it *does not represent* the working class. It must recognize itself as no more than a radical separation from *the world of separation.*

120

The revolutionary organization is the coherent expression of the theory of praxis entering into non-unilateral communication with practical struggles, in the process of becoming practical theory. Its own practice is the generalization of communication and of coherence in these struggles. At the revolutionary moment of dissolution of social separation, this organization must recognize its own dissolution as a separate organization.

121

The revolutionary organization can be nothing less than a unitary critique of society, namely a critique which does not compromise with any form of separate power anywhere in the world, and a critique proclaimed globally against all the aspects of alienated social life. In the struggle between the revolutionary organization and class society, the weapons are nothing other than the *essence* of the combatants themselves: the revolutionary organization cannot reproduce within itself the dominant society's conditions of separation and hierarchy. It must struggle constantly against its deformation in the ruling spectacle. The only limit to participation in the total democracy of the revolutionary organization is the recognition and self-appropriation of the coherence of its critique by all its members, a coherence which must be proved in the critical theory as such and in the relation between the theory and practical activity.

122

When constantly growing capitalist alienation at all levels makes it increasingly difficult for workers to recognize and name their own misery, forcing them to face the alternative of rejecting *the totality of their misery or nothing,* the revolutionary organization has to learn that it can no longer *combat alienation with alienated forms.*

123

Proletarian revolution depends entirely on the condition that, for the first time, theory as intelligence of human practice be recognized and lived by the masses. It requires workers to become dialecticians and to inscribe their thought into practice. Thus it demands of *men without quality* more than the bourgeois revolution demanded of the qualified men which it delegated to carry out its tasks (since the partial ideological consciousness constructed by a part of the bourgeois class was based on the economy, this central *part* of social life in which this class *was already in power*). The very development of class society to the stage of spectacular organization of non-life thus leads the revolutionary project to become *visibly* what it already was *essentially.*

124

Revolutionary theory is now the enemy of all revolutionary ideology *and knows it.*

V

Time and History

O, gentlemen, the time of life is short! . . .
And if we live, we live to tread on kings . . .

—Shakespeare, *Henry IV*

Man, "the negative being who is only to the extent that he suppresses Being," is identical to time. Man's appropriation of his own nature is at the same time his grasp of the unfolding of the universe. "History is itself a real part of *natural history*, of the transformation of nature into man" (Marx). Inversely, this "natural history" has no actual existence other than through the process of human history, the only part which recaptures this historical totality, like the modern telescope whose sight captures, *in time*, the retreat of nebulae at the periphery of the universe. History has always existed, but not always in a historical form. The temporalization of man as effected through the mediation of a society is equivalent to a humanization of time. The unconscious movement of time manifests itself and *becomes true* within historical consciousness.

126

Properly historical movement, although still hidden, begins in the slow and intangible formation of the "real nature of man," this "nature born within human history—within the generating action of human society—," but even though that society developed a technology and a language and is already a product of its own history, it is conscious only of a perpetual present. There, all knowledge, confined within the memory of the oldest, is always carried by the *living*. Neither death nor procreation is grasped as a law of time. Time remains immobile, like an enclosed space. A more complex society which finally becomes conscious of time devotes itself to negating it because it sees in time not what passes, but only what returns. A static society organizes time in terms of its immediate experience of nature, on the model of *cyclical* time.

127

Cyclical time already dominates the experience of nomadic populations because they find the same conditions repeated at every moment of their journey: Hegel notes that "the wandering of nomads is only formal because it is limited to uniform spaces." The society which, by fixing itself in place locally, gives space a content by arranging individualized places, thus finds itself enclosed inside this localization. The temporal return to similar places now becomes the pure return of time in the same place, the repetition of a series of gestures. The transition from pastoral nomadism to sedentary agriculture is the end of the lazy liberty without content, the beginning of labor. The agrarian mode of production in general, dominated by the rhythm of the seasons, is the basis for fully constituted cyclical time. Eternity is *internal* to it; it is the return of the same here on earth. Myth is the unitary construction of the thought which guarantees the entire cosmic order surrounding the order which this society has in fact already realized within its frontiers.

128

The social appropriation of time, the production of man by human labor, develops within a society divided into classes. The power which constituted itself above the penury of the society of cyclical time, the class which organizes the social labor and appropriates the limited surplus value, simultaneously appropriates the *temporal surplus value* of its organization of social time: it possesses for itself alone the irreversible time of the living. The wealth that can be concentrated in the realm of power and materially used up in sumptuous feasts is also used up as a squandering of *historical time at the surface of society*. The owners of historical surplus value possess the knowledge and the enjoyment of lived events. Separated from the collective organization of time which predominates with the repetitive production at the base of social life, this time flows above its own static community. This is the time of adventure and war, when the masters of the cyclical society travel through their personal histories, and it is also the time which appears in confrontations with foreign communities, in the derangement of the unchangeable order of the society. History then passes before men as an alien factor, as that which they never wanted and against which they thought themselves protected. But by way of this detour returns the human negative *anxiety* which had been at the very origin of the entire development that had fallen asleep.

129

Cyclical time in itself is time without conflict. But conflict is installed within this infancy of time: history first struggles to be history in the practical activity of masters. This history superficially creates the irreversible; its movement constitutes precisely the time it uses up within the interior of the inexhaustible time of cyclical society.

130

"Frozen societies" are those which slowed down their historical activity to the limit and maintained in constant equilibrium their opposition to the natural and human environment as well as their internal oppositions. If the extreme diversity of institutions established for this purpose demonstrates the flexibility of the self-creation of human nature, this demonstration becomes obvious only for the external observer, for the anthropologist who returns from historical time. In each of these societies a definitive structuring excluded change. Absolute conformism in existing social practices, with which all human possibilities are identified for all time, has no external limit other than the fear of falling back into formless animality. Here, in order to remain human, men must remain the same.

131

The birth of political power which seems to be related to the last great technological revolutions (like iron smelting), at the threshold of a period which would not experience profound shocks until the appearance of industry, also marks the moment when kinship ties begin to dissolve. From then on, the succession of generations leaves the sphere of pure cyclical nature in order to become an event-oriented succession of powers. Irreversible time is now the time of those who rule, and dynasties are its first measure. Writing is its weapon. In writing, language attains its complete independent reality as mediation between consciousnesses. But this independence is identical to the general independence of separate power as the mediation which constitutes society. With writing there appears a consciousness which is no longer carried and transmitted directly among the living: an *impersonal memory*, the memory of the administration of society. "Writings are the thoughts of the State; archives are its memory" (Novalis).

The chronicle is the expression of the irreversible time of power and also the instrument that preserves the voluntaristic progression of this time from its predecessor, since this orientation of time collapses with the fall of every specific power and returns to the indifferent oblivion of cyclical time, the only time known to peasant masses who, during the collapse of empires and their chronologies, never change. The *owners of history* have given time *a meaning*: a direction which is also a significance. But this history deploys itself and succumbs separately, leaving the underlying society unchanged precisely because this history remains separated from the common reality. This is why we reduce the history of Oriental empires to the history of religions: the chronologies which have fallen to ruins left no more than the apparently autonomous history of the illusions which enveloped them. The masters who *make history their private property*, under the protection of myth, possess first of all a private ownership of the mode of illusion: in China and Egypt they long held a monopoly over the immortality of the soul, just as their famous early dynasties are imaginary arrangements of the past. But the masters' possession of illusion is at that moment the only possible possession of a common history and of their own history. The growth of their real historical power goes together with a popularization of the possession of myth and illusion. All this flows from the simple fact that, to the extent that the masters took it upon themselves to guarantee the permanence of cyclical time mythically, as in the seasonal rites of Chinese emperors, they themselves achieved a relative liberation from cyclical time.

The dry unexplained chronology of divine power speaking to its servants, which wants to be understood only as the earthly execution of the commandments of myth, can be surmounted and become conscious history; this requires that real participation in history be lived by extended groups. Out of this practical communication among those who *recognized each other* as possessors of a singular present, who experienced the qualitative richness of events as their activity and as the place where they lived—their epoch—arises the general language of historical communication. Those for whom irreversible time has existed discover within it the *memorable* as well as the *menace of forgetting:* "Herodotus of Halicarnassus here presents the results of his study, so that time may not abolish the works of men . . ."

134

Reasoning about history is inseparably *reasoning about power.* Greece was the moment when power and its change were discussed and understood, the *democracy of the masters* of society. Greek conditions were the inverse of the conditions known to the despotic State, where power settles its accounts only with itself within the inaccessible obscurity of its densest point: through *palace revolution*, which is placed beyond the pale of discussion by success or failure alike. However, the power shared among the Greek communities existed only with the *expenditure* of a social life whose production remained separate and static within the servile class. Only those who do not work live. In the division among the Greek communities, and in the struggle to exploit foreign cities, the principle of separation which internally grounded each of them was externalized. Greece, which had dreamed of universal history, did not succeed in unifying itself in the face of invasion—or even in unifying the calendars of its independent cities. In Greece historical time became conscious, but not yet conscious of itself.

135

After the disappearance of the locally favorable conditions known to the Greek communities, the regression of western historical thought was not accompanied by a rehabilitation of ancient mythic organizations. Out of the confrontations of the Mediterranean populations, out of the formation and collapse of the Roman State, appeared *semi-historical religions* which became fundamental factors in the new consciousness of time, and in the new armor of separate power.

136

The monotheistic religions were a compromise between myth and history, between cyclical time which still dominated production and irreversible time where populations clash and regroup. The religions which grew out of Judaism are abstract universal acknowledgements of irreversible time which is democratized, opened to all, but in the realm of illusion. Time is totally oriented toward a single final event: "The Kingdom of God is at hand." These religions arose on the soil of history, and established themselves there. But there they still preserve themselves in radical opposition to history. Semi-historical religion establishes a qualitative point of departure in time (the birth of Christ, the flight of Mohammed), but its irreversible time—introducing real accumulation which in Islam can take the form of a conquest, or in Reformation Christianity the form of increased capital—is actually inverted in religious thought and becomes a *count-down*: the hope of access to the genuine other world before time runs out, the expectation of the last Judgment. Eternity came out of cyclical time and is beyond it. Eternity is the element which holds back the irreversibility of time, suppressing history within history itself by placing itself *on the other side of irreversible time* as a pure punctual element to which cyclical time returned and abolished itself. Bossuet will still say: "And by means of the time that passes we enter into the eternity which does not pass."

137

The Middle Ages, this incomplete mythical world whose perfection lay outside it, is the moment when cyclical time, which still regulates the greater part of production, is really chewed away by history. A certain irreversible temporality is recognized individually in everyone, in the succession of stages of life, in the consideration of life as a *journey*, a passage with no return through a world whose meaning lies elsewhere: the *pilgrim* is the man who leaves cyclical time and becomes in reality the traveller that everyone is symbolically. Personal historical life still finds its fulfillment within the sphere of power, within participation in struggles led by power and in struggles over disputed power; but the irreversible time of power is shared to infinity under the general unification of the oriented time of the Christian era, in a world of *armed faith*, where the game of the masters revolves around fidelity and disputes over owed fidelity. This feudal society, born out of the encounter of "the organizational structure of the conquering army as it developed during the conquest" with "the productive forces found in the conquered country" (*German Ideology*)—and in the organization of these productive forces one must count their religious language—divided the domination of society between the Church and the state power, in turn subdivided in the complex relations of suzereinty and vassalage of territorial tenures and urban communes. In this diversity of possible historical life, the irreversible time which silently carried off the underlying society, the time lived by the bourgeoisie in the production of commodities, in the foundation and expansion of cities and in the commercial discovery of the earth—practical experimentation which forever destroyed all mythical organization of the cosmos—slowly revealed itself as the unknown work of this epoch when the great official historical undertaking of this world collapsed with the Crusades.

138

During the decline of the Middle Ages, the irreversible time which invades society is experienced by the consciousness attached to the ancient order in the form of an obsession with death. This is the melancholy of the demise of a world, the last world where the security of myth still counterpoised history, and for this melancholy everything worldly moves only toward corruption. The great revolts of the European peasants are also their attempt *to respond to history*—which was violently wrenching the peasants out of the patriarchal sleep that had guaranteed their feudal tutelage. This millenarian utopia of *achieving heaven on earth* revives what was at the origin of semi-historical religion, when Christian communities which grew out of Judaic messianism responded to the troubles and unhappiness of the epoch by looking to the imminent realization of the Kingdom of God and brought a disquieting and subversive factor into ancient society. When Christianity reached the point of sharing power within the empire, it exposed what still survived of this hope as a simple superstition: that is the meaning of the Augustinian affirmation, archetype of all the *satisfecit* of modern ideology, according to which the established Church has already for a long time been this kingdom one spoke of. The social revolt of the millenarian peasantry defines itself naturally first of all as a will to destroy the Church. But millenarianism spreads in the historical world, and not on the terrain of myth. Modern revolutionary expectations are not irrational continuations of the religious passion of millenarianism, as Norman Cohn thought he had demonstrated in *The Pursuit of the Millenium*. On the contrary, it is millenarianism, revolutionary class struggle speaking the language of religion for the last time, which is already a modern revolutionary tendency that as yet lacks *the consciousness that it is only historical.* The millenarians had to lose because they could not recognize the revolution as their own operation. The fact that they waited to act on the basis of an external sign of God's decision is the translation into thought of the practice of insurgent peasants following chiefs taken from outside their ranks. The peasant class could not attain an adequate consciousness of the functioning of society or of the way to lead its own struggle; because it lacked these conditions of unity in its action and consciousness, it expressed its project and led its wars with the imagery of an earthly paradise.

139

The new possession of historical life, the Renaissance, which finds its past and its legitimacy in Antiquity, carries with it a joyous rupture with eternity. Its irreversible time is that of the infinite accumulation of knowledge, and the historical consciousness which grows out of the experience of democratic communities and of the forces which ruin them will take up, with Machiavelli, the analysis of desanctified power, saying the unspeakable about the State. In the exuberant life of the Italian cities, in the art of the festival, life is experienced as enjoyment of the passage of time. But this enjoyment of passage is itself a passing enjoyment. The song of Lorenzo di Medici considered by Burckhardt to be the expression of "the very spirit of the Renaissance" is the eulogy which this fragile feast of history pronounces on itself: "How beautiful the spring of life—which vanishes so quickly."

140

The constant movement of monopolization of historical life by the State of the absolute monarchy, transitional form toward complete domination by the bourgeois class, brings into clear view the new irreversible time of the bourgeoisie. The bourgeoisie is attached to *labor time,* which is liberated for the first time from the cyclical. With the bourgeoisie, work becomes *labor which transforms historical conditions.* The bourgeoisie is the first ruling class for which labor is a value. And the bourgeoisie which suppresses all privilege, which recognizes no value that does not flow from the exploitation of labor, has justly identified with labor its own value as a dominant class, and has made the progress of labor its own progress.

The class which accumulates commodities and capital continually modifies nature by modifying labor itself, by unleashing its productivity. All social life has already been concentrated within the ornamental poverty of the Court, the tinsel of the cold state administration which culminates in "the vocation of king"; and all particular historical liberty has had to consent to its defeat. The liberty of the irreversible temporal game of the nobles is consumed in their last lost battles, the wars of the Fronde and the rising of the Scotch for Charles-Edward. The world's foundation has changed.

141

The victory of the bourgeoisie is the victory of *profoundly historical* time, because this is the time of economic production which transforms society, continuously and from top to bottom. So long as agrarian production remains the central activity, the cyclical time which remains at the base of society nourishes the coalesced forces of *tradition* which fetter all movement. But the irreversible time of the bourgeois economy eradicates these vestiges on every corner of the globe. History, which until then had seemed to be only the movement of individuals of the ruling class, and thus was written as the history of events, is now understood as the *general movement*, and in this relentless movement individuals are sacrificed. This history which discovers its foundation in political economy now knows of the existence of what had been its unconscious, but this still cannot be brought to light and remains unconscious. This blind prehistory, a new fatality dominated by no one, is all that the commodity economy democratized.

142

The history which is present in all the depths of society tends to be lost at the surface. The triumph of irreversible time is also its metamorphosis into the *time of things*, because the weapon of its victory was precisely the mass production of objects according to the laws of the commodity. The main product which economic development has transferred from luxurious scarcity to daily consumption is therefore *history*, but only in the form of the history of the abstract movement of things which dominates all qualitative use of life. While the earlier cyclical time had supported a growing part of historical time lived by individuals and groups, the domination of the irreversible time of production tends, socially, to eliminate this lived time.

143

Thus the bourgeoisie made known to society and imposed on it an irreversible historical time, but kept its *use* from society. "There was history, but there is no more," because the class of owners of the economy, which cannot break with *economic history*, is directly threatened by all other irreversible use of time and must repress it. The ruling class, made up of *specialists in the possession of things* who are themselves therefore a possession of things, must link its fate with the preservation of this reified history, with the permanence of a new immobility *within history*. For the first time the worker, at the base of society, is not materially a *stranger to history*, because it is now the base that irreversibly moves society. In the demand to *live* the historical time which it makes, the proletariat finds the simple unforgettable center of its revolutinary project; and every attempt (thwarted until now) to realize this project marks a point of possible departure for new historical life.

144

The irreversible time of the bourgeoisie in power at first presented itself under its own name, as an absolute origin, Year One of the Republic. But the revolutionary ideology of general freedom which had destroyed the last remnants of the mythical organization of values and the entire traditional regulation of society, already made visible the real will which it had clothed in Roman dress: *the freedom of generalized commerce*. The commodity society, now discovering that it needed to reconstruct the passivity which it had profoundly shaken in order to set up its own pure reign, finds that "Christianity with its *cultus* of abstract man ... is the most fitting form of religion" (*Capital*). Thus the bourgeoisie establishes a compromise with this religion, a compromise which also expresses itself in the presentation of time: its own calendar abandoned, its irreversible time returns to unwind within the Christian era whose succession it continues.

145

With the development of capitalism, irreversible time is *unified on a world scale.* Universal history becomes a reality because the entire world is gathered under the development of this time. But this history, which is everywhere simultaneously the same, is still only the refusal within history of history itself. What appears the world over as *the same day* is the time of economic production cut up into equal abstract fragments. Unified irreversible time is the time of the *world market* and, as a corollary, of the world spectacle.

146

The irreversible time of production is first of all the measure of commodities. Therefore the time officially affirmed over the entire expanse of the globe as the *general time of society* refers only to the specialized interests which constitute it and *is no more than a particular time.*

VI

Spectacular Time

We have nothing of our own but time, which is enjoyed precisely by those who have no place to stay.

—Baltasar Gracian, *L'Homme de cour*

The time of production, commodity-time, is an infinite ac-cumulation of equivalent intervals. It is the abstraction of ir-reversible time, all of whose segments must prove on the chronometer their merely quantitative equality. This time is in reality exactly what it is in its *exchangeable* character. In this social domination by commodity-time, "time is everything, man is nothing; he is at most the carcass of time" (*Poverty of Philosophy*). This is time devalued, the complete inversion of time as "the field of human development."

148

The general time of human non-development also exists in the complementary form of *consumable time* which returns as *pseudo-cyclical time* to the daily life of the society based on this determined production.

149

Pseudo-cyclical time is actually no more than the *consumable disguise* of the commodity-time of production. It contains the essential properties of commodity-time, namely exchangeable homogeneous units and the suppression of the qualitative dimension. But being the by-product of this time which aims to retard concrete daily life and to keep it retarded, it must be charged with pseudo-valuations and appear in a sequence of falsely individualized moments.

150

Pseudo-cyclical time is the time of consumption of modern economic survival, of increased survival, where daily life con-tinues to be deprived of decision and remains bound, no longer to the natural order, but to the pseudo-nature developed in alienated labor; and thus this time *naturally* reestablishes the ancient cyclical rhythm which regulated the survival of pre-industrial societies. Pseudo-cyclical time leans on the natural remains of cyclical time and also uses it to compose new homologous combinations: day and night, work and weekly rest, the recurrence of vacations.

Pseudo-cyclical time is a time *transformed by industry*. The time which has its basis in the production of commodities is itself a consumable commodity which includes everything that previously (during the phase of dissolution of the old unitary society) was differentiated into private life, economic life, political life. All the consumable time of modern society comes to be treated as a raw material for varied new products which impose themselves on the market as uses of socially organized time. "A product which already exists in a form which makes it suitable for consumption can nevertheless in its turn become a raw material for another product" (*Capital*).

In its most advanced sector, concentrated capitalism orients itself towards the sale of "completely equipped" blocks of time, each one constituting a single unified commodity which integrates a number of diverse commodities. In the expanding economy of "services" and leisure, this gives rise to the formula of calculated payment in which "everything's included": spectacular environment, the collective pseudo-displacement of vacations, subscriptions to cultural consumption, and the sale of sociability itself in the form of "passionate conversations" and "meetings with personalities." This sort of spectacular commodity, which can obviously circulate only because of the increased poverty of the corresponding realities, just as obviously fits among the pilot-articles of modernized sales techniques by being payable on credit.

Consumable pseudo-cyclical time is spectacular time, both as the time of consumption of images in the narrow sense, and as the image of consumption of time in the broad sense. The time of image-consumption, the medium of all commodities, is inseparably the field where the instruments of the spectacle exert themselves fully, and also their goal, the location and main form of all specific consumption: it is known that the time-saving constantly sought by modern society, whether in the speed of vehicles or in the use of dried soups, is concretely translated for the population of the United States in the fact that the mere contemplation of television occupies it for an average of three to six hours a day. The social image of the consumption of time, in turn, is exclusively dominated by moments of leisure and vacation, moments presented *at a distance* and desirable by definition, like every spectacular commodity. Here this commodity is explicitly presented as the moment of real life, and the point is to wait for its cyclical return. But even in those very moments reserved for living, it is still the spectacle that is to be seen and reproduced, becoming ever more intense. What was represented as genuine life reveals itself simply as more *genuinely spectacular* life.

154

The epoch which displays its time to itself as essentially the sudden return of multiple festivities is also an epoch without festivals. What was, in cyclical time, the moment of a community's participation in the luxurious expenditure of life is impossible for the society without community or luxury. When its vulgarized pseudo-festivals, parodies of the dialogue and the gift, incite a surplus of economic expenditure, they lead only to deception always compensated by the promise of a new deception. In the spectacle, the lower the use value of modern survival-time, the more highly it is exalted. The reality of time has been replaced by the *advertisement* of time.

While the consumption of cyclical time in ancient societies was consistent with the real labor of those societies, the pseudo-cyclical consumption of the developed economy is in contradiction with the abstract irreversible time of its production. While cyclical time was the time of immobile illusion, really lived, spectacular time is the time of self-changing reality, lived in illusion.

156

What is constantly new in the process of production of things is not found in consumption, which remains the expanded repetition of the same. In spectacular time, since dead labor continues to dominate living labor, the past dominates the present.

157

Another side of the deficiency of general historical life is that individual life as yet has no history. The pseudo-events which rush by in spectacular dramatizations have not been lived by those informed of them; moreover they are lost in the inflation of their hurried replacement at every throb of the spectacular machinery. Furthermore, what is really lived has no relation to the official irreversible time of society and is in

direct opposition to the pseudo-cyclical rhythm of the consumable by-product of this time. This individual experience of separate daily life remains without language, without concept, without critical access to its own past which has been recorded nowhere. It is not communicated. It is not understood and is forgotten to the profit of the false spectacular memory of the unmemorable.

158

The spectacle, as the present social organization of the paralysis of history and memory, of the abandonment of history built on the foundation of historical time, is the *false consciousness of time*.

159

The preliminary condition required for propelling workers to the status of "free" producers and consumers of commodity time was *the violent expropriation of their own time*. The spectacular return of time became possible only after this first dispossession of the producer.

160

The irreducibly biological element which remains in labor, both in the dependence on the natural cycle of waking and sleep and in the existence of irreversible time in the expenditure of an individual life, is a mere *accessory* from the point of view of modern production; consequently, these elements are ignored in the official proclamations of the movement of production and in the consumable trophies which are the accessible translation of this incessant victory. The spectator's consciousness, immobilized in the falsified center of the movement of its world, no longer experiences its life as a passage toward self-realization and toward death. One who has renounced using his life can no longer admit his death. Life insurance advertisements suggest merely that he is guilty of dying without ensuring the regularity of the system after this economic loss; and the advertisement of the *American way of death* insists on his capacity to maintain in this encounter the greatest possible number of *appearances* of life. On all other fronts of the advertising onslaught, it is strictly forbidden to grow old. Even a "youth-capital," contrived for each and all and put to the most mediocre uses, could never acquire the durable and cumulative reality of financial capital. This social absence of death is identical to the social absence of life.

161

Time, as Hegel showed, is the *necessary* alienation, the environment where the subject realizes himself by losing himself, where he becomes other in order to become truly himself. Precisely the opposite is true in the dominant alienation, which is undergone by the producer of an *alien present*. In this *spatial alienation*, the society that radically separates the subject from the activity it takes from him, separates him first of all from his own time. It is this surmountable social alienation that has prohibited and petrified the possibilities and risks of the *living* alienation of time.

162

Under the visible *fashions* which disappear and reappear on the trivial surface of contemplated pseudo-cyclical time, the *grand style* of the age is always located in what is oriented by the obvious and secret necessity of revolution.

163

The natural basis of time, the actual experience of the flow of time, becomes human and social by existing *for man*. The restricted condition of human practice, labor at various stages, is what has humanized and also dehumanized time as cyclical and as separate irreversible time of economic production. The revolutionary project of realizing a classless society, a generalized historical life, is the project of a withering away of the social measure of time, to the benefit of a playful model of irreversible time of individuals and groups, a model in which *independent federated times* are simultaneously present. It is the program of a total realization, within the context of time, of communism which suppresses "all that exists independently of individuals."

164

The world already possesses the dream of a time whose consciousness it must now possess in order to actually live it.

VII

The Organization of Territory

And whoever becomes ruler of a city accustomed to living freely and does not destroy it, let him expect to be destroyed by her, because as refuge for her rebellions she always has the name of liberty and her old customs, which neither through the length of time nor for any good deed will ever be forgotten. And whatever one does there and whatever one provides, if it is not to persecute or disperse the inhabitants, this name and these customs will never be forgotten.

—Machiavelli, *The Prince*

Capitalist production has unified space, which is no longer bounded by external societies. This unification is at the same time an extensive and intensive process of *banalization*. The accumulation of commodities produced in mass for the abstract space of the market, which had to break down all regional and legal barriers and all the corporative restrictions of the Middle Ages that preserved the *quality* of craft production, also had to destroy the autonomy and quality of places. This power of homogenization is the heavy artillery which brought down all Chinese walls.

166

In order to become ever more identical to itself, to get as close as possible to motionless monotony, *the free space of the commodity* is henceforth constantly modified and reconstructed.

167

This society which eliminates geographical distance reproduces distance internally as spectacular separation.

168

Tourism, human circulation considered as consumption, a by-product of the circulation of commodities, is fundamentally nothing more than the leisure of going to see what has become banal. The economic organization of visits to different places is already in itself the guarantee of their *equivalence*. The same modernization that removed time from the voyage also removed from it the reality of space.

169

The society that molds all of its surroundings has developed a special technique for shaping its very territory, the solid ground of this collection of tasks. Urbanism is capitalism's seizure of the natural and human environment;

developing logically into absolute domination, capitalism can and must now remake the totality of space into *its own setting*.

170

The capitalist need which is satisfied by urbanism in the form of a visible freezing of life can be expressed in Hegelian terms as the absolute predominance of "the peaceful coexistence of space" over "the restless becoming in the passage of time."

171

If all the technical forces of capitalism must be understood as tools for the making of separations, in the case of urbanism we are dealing with the equipment at the basis of these technical forces, with the treatment of the ground that suits their deployment, with the very technique *of separation*.

172

Urbanism is the modern fulfillment of the uninterrupted task which safeguards class power: the preservation of the atomization of workers who had been dangerously *brought together* by urban conditions of production. The constant struggle that had to be waged against every possible form of their coming together discovers its favored field in urbanism. After the experiences of the French Revolution, the efforts of all established powers to increase the means of maintaining order in the streets finally culminates in the suppression of the street. "With the present means of long-distance mass communication, sprawling isolation has proved an even more effective method of keeping a population under control," says Lewis Mumford in *The City in History*, describing "henceforth a one-way world." But the general movement of isolation, which is the reality of urbanism, must also include a controlled reintegration of workers depending on the needs of production and consumption that can be planned. Integration into the system requires that isolated individuals be recaptured and *isolated together*: factories and halls of culture, tourist resorts and housing developments are expressly organized to serve this pseudo-community that follows the isolated individual right into the *family cell*. The widespread use of receivers of the spectacular message enables the individual to fill his isolation with the dominant images—images which derive their power precisely from this isolation.

173

For the first time a new architecture, which in all previous epochs had been reserved for the satisfaction of the ruling classes, is directly aimed *at the poor*. The formal poverty and the gigantic spread of this new living experience both come from its *mass* character, which is implicit in its purpose and in modern conditions of construction. *Authoritarian decision*, which abstractly organizes territory into territory of abstraction, is obviously at the heart of these modern conditions of construction. The same architecture appears in all industrializing countries that are backward in this respect, as a suitable terrain for the new type of social existence which is to be implanted there. The threshold crossed by the growth of society's material power alongside the *lag* in the conscious domination of this power, are displayed as clearly by urbanism as by problems of thermonuclear armament or of birth control (where the possibility of manipulating heredity has already been reached).

The present is already the time of the self-destruction of the urban milieu. The explosion of cities which cover the countryside with "formless masses of urban residues" (Lewis Mumford) is directly regulated by the imperatives of consumption. The dictatorship of the automobile, pilot-product of the first phase of commodity abundance, has been stamped into the environment with the domination of the freeway, which dislocates old urban centers and requires an ever-larger dispersion. At the same time, stages of incomplete reorganization of the urban fabric polarize temporarily around "distribution factories," enormous shopping centers built on the bare ground of parking lots; and these temples of frenzied consumption, after bringing about a partial rearrangement of congestion, themselves flee within the centrifugal movement which rejects them as soon as they in turn become overburdened secondary centers. But the technical organization of consumption is only the first element of the general dissolution which has led the city to the point of *consuming itself.*

175

Economic history, which developed entirely around the opposition between town and country, has reached a level of

success which simultaneously cancels out both terms. The current *paralysis* of total historical development for the sake of the mere continuation of the economy's independent movement makes the moment when town and country begin to disappear, not the *supersession* of their cleavage, but their simultaneous collapse. The reciprocal erosion of town and country, product of the failure of the historical movement through which existing urban reality should have been surmounted, is visible in the eclectic melange of their decayed elements which cover the most industrially advanced zones.

176

Universal history was born in cities and reached maturity at the moment of the decisive victory of city over country. To Marx, one of the greatest revolutionary merits of the bourgeoisie was "the subjection of the country to the city" whose very *air emancipates*. But if the history of the city is the history of freedom, it is also the history of tyranny, of state administration that controls the countryside and the city itself. The city could as yet only struggle for historical freedom, but not possess it. The city is the *locus of history* because it is conscious of the past and also concentrates the social power that makes the historical undertaking possible. The present tendency to liquidate the city is thus merely another expression of the delay in the subordination of the economy to historical consciousness and in the unification of society reassuming the powers that were detached from it.

177

"The countryside shows the exact opposite: isolation and separation" (*German Ideology*). Urbanism destroys cities and reestablishes a *pseudo-countryside* which lacks the natural relations of the old countryside as well as the direct social relations which were directly challenged by the historical city. A new artificial peasantry is recreated by the conditions of housing and spectacular control in today's "organized territory": the geographic dispersal and narrowmindedness that always kept the peasantry from undertaking independent action and from affirming itself as a creative historical force again today become characteristics of the producers—the movement of a world which they themselves produce remaining as completely beyond their reach as the natural rhythm of tasks was for the agrarian society. But when this peasantry, which was the unshakable foundation of "Oriental despotism" and whose very fragmentation called for bureaucratic centralization, reemerges as a product of the conditions of growth of modern state bureaucracy, its *apathy* must now be *historically manufactured* and maintained; natural ignorance has been replaced by the organized spectacle of error. The "new towns" of the technological pseudo-peasantry clearly inscribe on the landscape their rupture with the historical time on which they are built; their motto could be: "On this spot nothing will ever happen, and *nothing ever has.*" It is obviously because history, which must be liberated in the cities, has not yet been liberated, that the forces of *historical absence* begin to compose their own exclusive landscape.

178

History, which threatens this twilight world, is also the force which could subject space to lived time. Proletarian revolution is the *critique of human geography* through which individuals and communities have to create places and events suitable for the appropriation, no longer just of their labor, but of their total history. In this game's changing space, and in the freely chosen variations in the game's rules, the autonomy of place can be rediscovered without the reintroduction of an exclusive attachment to the land, thus bringing back the reality of the voyage and of life understood as a voyage which contains its entire meaning within itself.

179

The greatest revolutionary idea concerning urbanism is not itself urbanistic, technological or esthetic. It is the decision to reconstruct the entire environment in accordance with the needs of the power of the Workers' Councils, of the *anti-statist dictatorship* of the proletariat, of enforceable dialogue. And the power of the Councils, which can be effective only if it transforms existing conditions in their entirety, cannot assign itself a smaller task if it wants to be recognized and *to recognize itself* in its world.

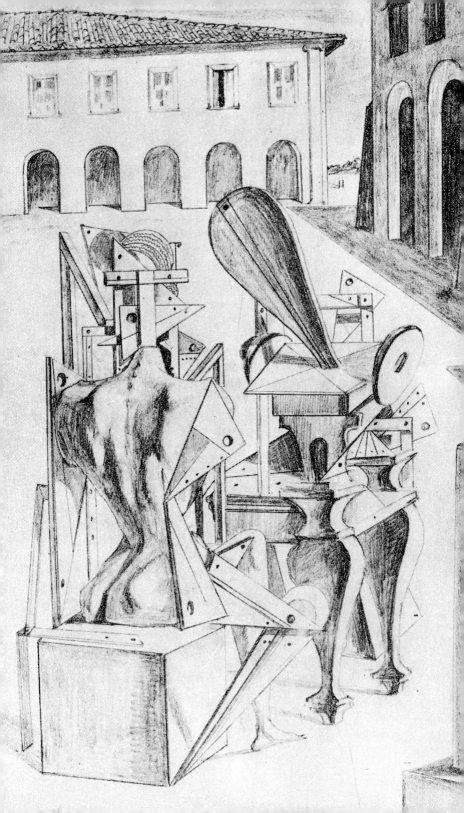

VIII

Negation and Consumption within Culture

Shall we live long enough to see a political revolution? We, the contemporaries of those Germans? My friend, you believe what you want to see ... As I judge Germany in terms of its present history, you cannot object that its whole history is falsified and all its present public life does not represent the real condition of the people. Read any newspaper you want, convince yourself that we don't stop—and you will concede that censorship prevents no one from stopping—to celebrate the liberty and national happiness we possess ...

—Ruge, *Letter to Marx*, March 1844

In the historical society divided into classes, culture is the general sphere of knowledge and of representations of the lived; which is to say that culture is the power of generalization existing *apart*, as division of intellectual labor and as intellectual labor of division. Culture detaches itself from the unity of the society of myth "when the power of unification disappears from the life of man and when opposites lose their living relation and interaction and acquire autonomy..." (Hegel's *Treatise on the Differences between the Systems of Fichte and Schelling*). By gaining its independence, culture begins an imperialist movement of enrichment which is at the same time the decline of its independence. The history which creates the relative autonomy of culture and the ideological illusions about this autonomy also expresses itself as history of culture. And the entire victorious history of culture can be understood as the history of the revelation of its inadequacy, as a march toward its self-suppression. Culture is the locus of the search for lost unity. In this search for unity, culture as a separate sphere is obliged to negate itself.

181

The struggle between tradition and innovation, which is the principle of internal cultural development in historical societies, can be carried on only through the permanent victory of innovation. Yet cultural innovation is carried by nothing other than the total historical movement which, by becoming conscious of its totality, tends to supersede its own cultural presuppositions and moves toward the suppression of all separation.

182

The growth of knowledge about society, which includes the understanding of history as the heart of culture, derives from itself an irreversible knowledge, which is expressed by the destruction of God. But this "first condition of any critique" is also the first obligation of a critique without end. When it is no longer possible to maintain a single rule of conduct, every *result* of culture forces culture to advance toward its dissolution. Like philosophy at the moment when it gained its full autonomy, every discipline which becomes autonomous has to collapse, first of all as a pretention to explain social totality coherently, and finally even as a fragmented tool which can be used within its own boundaries. The *lack of rationality* of separate culture is the element which condemns it to disappear, because within it the victory of the rational is already present as a requirement.

183

Culture grew out of the history which abolished the way of life of the old world, but as a separate sphere it is still no more than perceptible intelligence and communication, which remain partial in a *partially historical* society. It is the sense of a world which hardly makes sense.

184

The end of cultural history manifests itself on two opposite sides: the project of its supersession in total history, and the organization of its preservation as a dead object in spectacular contemplation. One of these movements has linked its fate to social critique, the other to the defense of class power.

185

The two sides of the end of culture—in all the aspects of knowledge as well as in all the aspects of perceptible representations—exist in a unified manner in what used to be *art* in the most general sense. In the case of knowledge, the accumulation of branches of fragmentary knowledge, which become unusable because the *approval* of existing conditions must finally renounce *knowledge of itself,* confronts the theory of praxis which alone holds the truth of them all since it alone holds the secret of their use. In the case of representations, the critical self-destruction of society's former *common language* confronts its artificial recomposition in the commodity spectacle, the illusory representation of the non-lived.

When society loses the community of the society of myth, it must lose all the references of a really common language until the time when the rifts within the inactive community can be surmounted by the inauguration of the real historical community. When art, which was the common language of social inaction, becomes independent art in the modern sense, emerging from its original religious universe and becoming individual production of separate works, it too experiences the movement that dominates the history of the entirety of separate culture. The affirmation of its independence is the beginning of its disintegration.

The loss of the language of communication is *positively* expressed by the modern movement of decomposition of all art, its formal annihilation. This movement expresses *negatively* the fact that a common language must be rediscovered—no longer in the unilateral conclusion which, in the art of the historical society, *always arrived too late*, speaking *to others* about what was lived without real dialogue, and admitting this deficiency of life—but it must be rediscovered in praxis, which unifies direct activity and its language. The problem is to actually possess the community of dialogue and the game with time which have been *represented* by poetico-artistic works.

When art, become independent, depicts its world in dazzling colors, a moment of life has grown old and it cannot be rejuvenated with dazzling colors. It can only be evoked as a memory. The greatness of art begins to appear only at the dusk of life.

The historical time which invades art expressed itself first of all in the sphere of art itself, starting with the *baroque*. Baroque is the art of a world which has lost its center: the last mythical order, in the cosmos and in terrestrial government, accepted by the Middle Ages—the unity of Christianity and the phantom of an Empire—has fallen. The *art of the change* must carry within itself the ephemeral principle it discovers in the world. It chose, said Eugenio d'Ors, "life against eternity." Theater and the festival, the theatrical festival, are the outstanding achievements of the baroque where every specific artistic expression becomes meaningful only with reference to the setting of a constructed place, a construction which is its own center of unification; this center is the *passage*, which is inscribed as a threatened equilibrium in the dynamic disorder of everything. The somewhat excessive importance given to the concept of the baroque in the contemporary discussion of esthetics is an expression of the awareness that artistic classicism is impossible: for three centuries the attempts to realize a normative classicism or neo-classicism were no more than brief artificial constructions speaking the external language of the State, the absolute monarchy, or the revolutionary bourgeoisie in Roman clothes. What followed the general path of the baroque, from romanticism to cubism, was ultimately an ever more individualized art of negation perpetually renewing itself to the point of the fragmentation and complete negation of the artistic sphere. The disappearance of historical art, which was linked to the internal communication of an elite and had its semi-independent social basis in the partly playful conditions still lived by the last aristocracies, also expresses the fact that capitalism possesses the first class power which admits itself stripped of any ontological quality, a power which, rooted in the simple management of the economy, is equally the loss of all human *mastery*. The baroque, artistic *creation's* long-lost unity, is in some way rediscovered in the current *consumption* of the totality of past art. When all past art is recognized and sought historically and retrospectively constituted into a world art, it is relativized into a global disorder which in turn constitutes a baroque edifice on a higher level, an edifice in which the very production of baroque art merges with all its revivals. The arts of all civilizations and all epochs can be known and accepted together for the first time. Once this "collection of souvenirs" of art history becomes possible, it is also *the end of the world of art.* In this age of museums, when artistic communication can no longer exist, all the former moments of art can be admitted equally, because they no longer suffer from the loss of their speficic conditions of communication in the current *general* loss of the conditions of communication.

As a negative movement which seeks the supersession of art in a historical society where history is not yet lived, art in the epoch of its dissolution is simultaneously an art of change and the pure expression of impossible change. The more grandiose its reach, the more its true realization is beyond it. This art is perforce *avant-garde*, and it *is not*. Its avant-garde is its disappearance.

Dadaism and surrealism are the two currents which mark the end of modern art. They are contemporaries, though only in a relatively conscious manner, of the last great assault of the revolutionary proletarian movement; and the defeat of this movement, which left them imprisoned in the same artistic field whose decrepitude they had announced, is the basic reason for their immobilization. Dadaism and surrealism are at once historically related and opposed to each other. This opposition, which each of them considered to be its most impor-

tant and radical contribution, reveals the internal inadequacy of their critique, which each developed one-sidedly. Dadaism wanted *to suppress art without realizing it;* surrealism wanted *to realize art without suppressing it.* The critical position later elaborated by the *Situationists* has shown that the suppression and the realization of art are inseparable aspects of a single *supersession of art.*

192

Spectacular consumption which preserves congealed past culture, including the recuperated repetition of its negative manifestations, openly becomes in the cultural sector what it is implicitly in its totality: the *communication of the incommunicable.* The flagrant destruction of language is flatly acknowledged as an officially positive value because the point is to advertise reconciliation with the dominant state of affairs —and here all communication is joyously proclaimed absent. The critical truth of this destruction—the real life of modern poetry and art—is obviously hidden, since the spectacle, whose function is *to make history forgotten within culture,* applies, in

the pseudo-novelty of its modernist means, the very strategy which constitutes its core. Thus a school of neo-literature, which simply admits that it contemplates the written word for its own sake, can present itself as something new. Furthermore, next to the simple proclamation of the sufficient beauty of the decay of the communicable, the most modern tendency of spectacular culture—and the one most closely linked to the repressive practice of the general organization of society—seeks to remake, by means of "team projects," a complex neo-artistic environment made up of decomposed elements: notably in urbanism's attempts to integrate artistic debris or esthetico-technical hybrids. This is an expression, on the level of spectacular pseudo-culture, of developed capitalism's general project, which aims to recapture the fragmented worker as a "personality well integrated in the group," a tendency described by American sociologists (Riesman, Whyte, etc.). It is the same project everywhere: *a restructuring without community*.

193

When culture becomes nothing more than a commodity, it must also become the star commodity of the spectacular society. Clark Kerr, one of the foremost ideologues of this tendency, has calculated that the complex process of production, distribution and consumption of *knowledge* already gets 29% of the yearly national product in the United States; and he predicts that in the second half of this century culture will be the driving force in the development of the economy, a role played by the automobile in the first half of this century, and by railroads in the second half of the previous century.

194

All the branches of knowledge, which continue to develop as the *thought of the spectacle*, have to justify a society without justification, and constitute a general science of false consciousness. This thought is completely conditioned by the fact that it cannot and will not investigate its own material basis in the spectacular system.

The system's thought, the thought of the social organization of appearance, is itself obscured by the generalized *sub-communication* which it defends. It does not know that conflict is at the origin of all things in its world. Specialists in the power of the spectacle, an absolute power within its system of language without response, are absolutely corrupted by their experience of contempt and of the success of contempt; and they find their contempt confirmed by their knowledge of *the contemptible man*, who the spectator really is.

Within the specialized thought of the spectacular system, a new division of tasks takes place to the extent that the improvement of this system itself poses new problems: on one hand, modern sociology which studies separation by means of the conceptual and material instruments of separation itself, undertakes the *spectacular critique of the spectacle;* on the other hand, in the various disciplines where structuralism takes root, the *apology for the spectacle* institutes itself as the thought of non-thought, as the *official amnesia* of historical practice. Nevertheless, the false despair of non-dialectical critique and the false optimism of pure advertising of the system are indentical in that they are both submissive thought.

The sociology which began, first in the United States, to focus discussion on the living conditions brought about by present development, compiled a great deal of empirical data, but could not fathom the truth of its subject because it lacked the critique immanent in this subject. As a result, the sincerely reformist tendency of this sociology resorts to morality, common sense, appeals devoid of all relevance to practical measures, etc. Because this type of critique is ignorant of the negative at the core of its world, it insists on describing only a sort of negative surplus which it finds deplorably annoying on the surface, like an irrational parasitic proliferation. This indignant good will, even if genuine, ends up blaming only the external consequences of the system, yet thinks itself critical, forgetting the essentially *apologetic* character of its assumptions and method.

Those who denounce the absurdity or the perils of incite-
ment to waste in the society of economic abundance do not
understand the purpose of waste. They condemn with in-
gratitude, in the name of economic rationality, the good irrational guardians without whom the power of this economic
rationality would collapse. For example, Boorstin, in *L'Image*,
describes the commercial consumption of the American spectacle but never reaches the concept of spectacle because he
thinks he can exempt private life, or the notion of "the honest
commodity," from this disastrous exaggeration. He does not
understand that the commodity itself made the laws whose
"honest" application leads to the distinct reality of private life
and to its subsequent reconquest by the social consumption of
images.

Boorstin describes the excesses of a world which has become foreign to us as if they were excesses foreign to our world.
But the "normal" basis of social life, to which he implicitly
refers when he characterizes the superficial reign of images
with psychological and moral judgments as a product of "our
extravagant pretentions," has no reality whatever, either in his
book or in his epoch. Boorstin cannot understand the full pro-
fundity of a society of images because the real human life he
speaks of is for him in the past, including the past of religious
resignation. The *truth* of this society is nothing other than the
negation of this society.

The sociology which thinks that an industrial rationality
functioning separately can be isolated from the whole of social
life can go so far as to isolate the techniques of reproduction
and transmission from the general industrial movement. Thus
Boorstin finds that the results he depicts are caused by the
unfortunate, almost fortuitous encounter of an oversized technical apparatus for image diffusion with an excessive attraction
to the pseudo-sensational on the part of the people of our
epoch. Thus the spectacle would be caused by the fact that
modern man is too much of a spectator. Boorstin fails to under-

stand that the proliferation of the prefabricated "pseudo-events" which he denounces flows from the simple fact that, in the massive reality of present social life, men do not themselves live events. Because history itself haunts modern society like a spectre, pseudo-histories are constructed at every level of consumption of life in order to preserve the threatened equilibrium of present *frozen time*.

201

The assertion of the definitive stability of a short period of frozen historical time is the undeniable basis, proclaimed consciously and unconsciously, of the present tendency toward a *structuralist* systematization. The vantage point from which anti-historical structuralist thought views the world is that of the eternal presence of a system which was never created and which will never end. The dream of the dictatorship of a pre-existing unconscious structure over all social praxis could be erroneously drawn from models of structures elaborated by linguistics and anthropology (and even the analysis of the functioning of capitalism)—models *already misunderstood in this context*—only because the academic imagination of *minor functionaries*, easily overwhelmed and completely entrenched in the awestruck celebration of the existing system, flatly reduces all reality to the existence of the system.

202

In order to understand "structuralist" categories, one must keep in mind, as with every historical social science, that the categories express forms as well as conditions of existence. Just as one cannot appraise the value of a man in terms of the conception he has of himself, one cannot appraise—and admire —this particular society by taking as indisputably true the language it speaks to itself; " . . .we cannot judge such epochs of transformation by their own consciousness; on the contrary, this consciousness must rather be explained in the light of the contradictions of material life . . ." Structure is the daughter of present power. Structuralism is the *thought guaranteed by the State* which regards the present conditions of spectacular "communication" as an absolute. Its method of studying the code of messages is itself nothing but the product, and the acknowledgement, of a society where communication exists in the form of a cascade of hierarchic signals. Consequently it is not structuralism which serves to prove the transhistorical validity of the society of the spectacle; it is on the contrary the society of the spectacle imposing itself as massive reality which serves to prove the cold dream of structuralism.

203

The critical concept of *spectacle* can undoubtedly also be vulgarized into a commonplace hollow formula of sociologico-political rhetoric to explain and abstractly denounce everything, and thus serve as a defense of the spectacular system. It is obvious that no idea can lead beyond the existing spectacle, but only beyond the existing ideas about the spectacle. To effectively destroy the society of the spectacle, what is needed is men putting a practical force into action. The critical theory of the spectacle can be true only by uniting with the practical current of negation in society, and this negation, the resumption of revolutionary class struggle, will become conscious of itself by developing the critique of the spectacle which is the theory of its real conditions (the practical conditions of present oppression), and inversely by unveiling the secret of what this negation can be. This theory does not expect miracles from the working class. It envisages the new formulation and the realization of proletarian imperatives as a long-range task. To make an artificial distinction between theoretical and practical struggle—since on the basis defined here, the very formulation and communication of such a theory cannot even be conceived without a *rigorous practice*—it is certain that the obscure and difficult path of critical theory must also be the lot of the practical movement acting on the scale of society.

204

Critical theory must be *communicated* in its own language. It is the language of contradiction, which must be dialectical in form as it is in content. It is critique of the totality and historical critique. It is not "the nadir of writing" but its inversion. It is not a negation of style, but the style of negation.

In its very style, the exposition of dialectical theory is a scandal and an abomination in terms of the rules and the corresponding tastes of the dominant language, because when it uses existing concrete concepts it is simultaneously aware of their rediscovered *fluidity*, their necessary destruction.

This style which contains its own critique must express the domination of the present critique *over its entire past*. The very mode of exposition of dialectical theory displays the negative spirit within it. "Truth is not like a product in which one can no longer find any trace of the tool that made it" (Hegel). This theoretical consciousness of movement, in which the movement's very trace must be evident, manifests itself by the *inversion* of the established relations between concepts and by the *diversion* of all the acquisitions of previous critique. The inversion of the genetive is this expression of historical revolutions, consigned to the form of thought, which was considered Hegel's epigrammatic style. The young Marx, recommending the technique Feuerbach had systematically used of replacing the subject with the predicate, achieved the most consistent use of this *insurrectional style*, drawing the misery of philosophy out of the philosophy of misery. Diversion leads to the subversion of past critical conclusions which were frozen into respectable truths, namely transformed into lies. Kierkegaard already used it deliberately, adding his own denunciation to it: "But despite all the tours and detours, just as jam always returns to the pantry, you always end up by sliding in a little word which isn't yours and which bothers you by the memory it awakens" *(Philosophical Fragments)*. It is the obligation of *distance* toward what was falsified into official truth which determines the use of diversion, as was acknowledged by Kierkegaard in the same book: "Only one more comment on your numerous allusions aiming at all the grief I mix into my statements of borrowed sayings. I do not deny it here nor will I deny that it was voluntary and that in a new continuation to this pamphlet, if I ever write it, I intend to name the object by its real name and to clothe the problem in historical attire."

Ideas improve. The meaning of words participates in the improvement. Plagiarism is necessary. Progress implies it. It embraces an author's phrase, makes use of his expressions, erases a false idea, and replaces it with the right idea.

Diversion is the opposite of quotation, of the theoretical authority which is always falsified by the mere fate of having become a quotation—a fragment torn from its context, from its movement, and ultimately from the global framework of its epoch and from the precise choice, whether exactly recognized or erroneous, which it was in this framework. Diversion is the fluid language of anti-ideology. It appears in communication which knows it cannot pretend to guarantee anything definitively and in itself. At its peak, it is language which cannot be confirmed by any former or supra-critical reference. On the contrary, its own coherence, in itself and with the applicable facts, can confirm the former core of truth which it brings out. Diversion has grounded its cause on nothing external to its own truth as present critique.

What openly presents itself as *diverted* in theoretical form, denying the durable autonomy of the sphere of the theoretically expressed by introducing there, *through this violence*, the action which upsets and overthrows the entire existing order, reminds us that the existence of theory is nothing in itself, and that it can know itself only through historical action and the *historical correction* which is its real counterpart.

Only the real negation of culture can preserve its meaning. It can no longer be *cultural*. Thus it is what in some way remains at the level of culture, but with a completely different meaning.

In the language of contradiction, the critique of culture presents itself as a *unified* critique in that it dominates the whole of culture, its knowledge as well as its poetry, and in that it no longer separates itself from the critique of the social totality. This *unified theoretical critique* goes alone to meet *unified social practice.*

IX

Ideology Materialized

Self-consciousness exists *in itself* and *for itself*
in that, and by the fact that it exists for another
self-consciousness; that is to say, it *is* only by
being acknowledged or recognized.

—Hegel, *Phenomenology of Mind*

Ideology is the *basis* of the thought of a class society in the conflict-laden course of history. Ideological facts were never a simple chimaera, but rather a deformed consciousness of realities, and in this form they have been real factors which set in motion real deforming acts; all the more so when the *materialization*, in the form of spectacle, of the ideology brought about by the concrete success of autonomized economic production in practice confounds social reality with an ideology which has tailored all reality in terms of its model.

When ideology, the *abstract* will—and the illusion—of the universal, is legitimized by the universal abstraction and the effective dictatorship of illusion in modern society, it is no longer a voluntaristic struggle of the partial, but its victory. At this point, ideological pretention acquires a sort of flat positivistic exactitude: it is no longer a historical choice but a fact. In this type of assertion, the particular *names* of ideologies have disappeared. Even the role of specifically ideological labor in the service of the system comes to be considered as nothing more than the recognition of an "epistemological base" that pretends to be beyond all ideological phenomena. Materialized ideology itself has no name, just as it has no expressible historical program. This is another way of saying that the history *of ideologies* is over.

Ideology, whose whole internal logic led to "total ideology" in Mannheim's sense—the despotism of the fragment which imposes itself as pseudo-knowledge of a frozen *totality, the totalitarian* vision—is now completed in the immobilized spectacle of non-history. Its completion is also its disintegration throughout society. With the *practical disintegration* of this society, ideology—the *final unreason* that blocks access to historical life—must disappear.

The spectacle is ideology par excellence, because it exposes and manifests in its fullness the essence of all ideological systems: the impoverishment, servitude and negation of real life. The spectacle is materially "the expression of the separation and estrangement between man and man." Through the "new power of fraud," concentrated at the base of the spectacle in this production, "the new domain of alien beings to whom man is subservient . . . grows coextensively with the mass of objects." It is the highest stage of an expansion which has turned need against life. "The need for money is thus the real need produced by political economy, and the only need it produces" (*Economic and Philosophical Manuscripts*). The spectacle extends to all social life the principle which Hegel (in the *Realphilosophie* of Jena) conceives as the principle of money: it is "the life of what is dead, moving within itself."

216

In opposition to the project summarized in the *Theses on Feuerbach* (the realization of philosophy in praxis which supersedes the opposition between idealism and materialism), the spectacle simultaneously preserves, and imposes within the pseudo-concrete of its universe, the ideological characteristics of materialism and idealism. The contemplative side of the old materialism which conceives the world as representation and not as activity—and which ultimately idealizes matter—is fulfilled in the spectacle, where concrete things are automatically the masters of social life. Reciprocally, the *dreamed activity* of idealism is equally fulfilled in the spectacle, through the technical mediation of signs and signals—which ultimately materialize an abstract ideal.

217

The parallel between ideology and schizophrenia, established by Gabel (*La Fausse Conscience*) must be placed in this economic process of materialization of ideology. Society has become what ideology already was. The removal of praxis and the anti-dialectical false consciousness which accompanies it are imposed during every hour of daily life subjected to the spectacle; this must be understood as a systematic organization of the "failure of the faculty of encounter" and as its replacement by a *hallucinatory social fact*: the false consciousness of encounter, the "illusion of encounter." In a society where no one can any longer be *recognized* by others, every individual becomes unable to recognize his own reality. Ideology is at home; separation has built its world.

218

"In clinical charts of schizophrenia," says Gabel, "the decay of the dialectic of totality (with dissociation as its extreme form) and the decay of the dialectic of becoming (with catatonia as its extreme form) seem solidly united." The spectator's consciousness, imprisoned in a flattened universe, bound by the *screen* of the spectacle behind which his life has been deported, knows only the *fictional speakers* who unilaterally surround him with their commodities and the politics of their commodities. The spectacle, in its entirety, is his "mirror image." Here the stage is set with the false exit of generalized autism.

219

The spectacle obliterates the boundaries between self and world by crushing the self besieged by the presence-absence of

the world and it obliterates the boundaries between true and false by driving all lived truth below the *real presence* of fraud ensured by the organization of appearance. One who passively accepts his alien daily fate is thus pushed toward a madness that reacts in an illusory way to this fate by resorting to magical techniques. The acceptance and consumption of commodities are at the heart of this pseudo-response to a communication without response. The need to imitate which is felt by the consumer is precisely the infantile need conditioned by all the aspects of his fundamental dispossession. In the terms applied by Gabel to a completely different pathological level, "the abnormal need for representation here compensates for a tortuous feeling of being on the margin of existence."

220

If the logic of false consciousness cannot know itself truly, the search for critical truth about the spectacle must simultaneously be a true critique. It must struggle in practice among the irreconcilable enemies of the spectacle and admit that it is absent where they are absent. The abstract desire for immediate effectiveness accepts the laws of the ruling thought, the exclusive point of view of the *present*, when it throws itself into reformist compromises or trashy pseudo-revolutionary common actions. Thus madness reappears in the very posture which pretends to fight it. Conversely, the critique which goes beyond the spectacle must *know how to wait.*

221

Emancipation from the material bases of inverted truth —this is what the self-emancipation of our epoch consists of. This "historical mission of installing truth in the world" cannot be accomplished either by the isolated individual, or by the atomized crowd subjected to manipulation, but now as ever by the class which is able to effect the dissolution of all classes by bringing all power into the dealienating form of realized democracy, the Council, in which practical theory controls itself and sees its own action. This is possible only where individuals are "directly linked to universal history"; only where dialogue arms itself to make its own conditions victorious.